Taxing Crime

Stolen Asset Recovery Initiative

The Stolen Asset Recovery Initiative (StAR) is a partnership between the World Bank Group and the United Nations Office on Drugs and Crime (UNODC) that supports international efforts to end safe havens for corrupt funds. StAR works with developing countries and financial centers to prevent the laundering of the corruption proceeds and to facilitate more systematic and timely return of stolen assets. For more information, visit https://star.worldbank.org/.

The StAR Initiative Series supports these efforts by providing practitioners with knowledge and policy tools that consolidate international good practice and wide-ranging practical experience on cutting-edge issues related to anticorruption and asset recovery efforts.

Previous Titles in the StAR Series

Asset Recovery Handbook: A Guide for Practitioners, second edition (2021) by Jean-Pierre Brun, Anastasia Sotiropoulou, Larissa Gray, Clive Scott, and Kevin M. Stephenson

Going for Broke: Insolvency Tools to Support Cross-Border Asset Recovery in Corruption Cases (2020) by Jean-Pierre Brun and Molly Silver

Getting the Full Picture on Public Officials: A How-to Guide for Effective Financial Disclosure (2017) by Ivana M. Rossi, Laura Pop, and Tammar Berger

Public Wrongs, Private Actions: Civil Lawsuits to Recover Stolen Assets (2015) by Jean-Pierre Brun, Pascale Helene Dubois, Emile van der Does de Willebois, Jeanne Hauch, Sarah Jaïs, Yannis Mekki, Anastasia Sotiropoulou, Katherine Rose Sylvester, and Mahesh Uttamchandani

Few and Far: The Hard Facts on Stolen Asset Recovery (2014) by Larissa Gray, Kjetil Hansen, Pranvera Recica-Kirkbride, and Linnea Mills

Left Out of the Bargain: Settlements in Foreign Bribery Cases and Implications for Asset Recovery (2014) by Jacinta Anyango Oduor, Francisca M. U. Fernando, Agustin Flah, Dorothee Gottwald, Jeanne M. Hauch, Marianne Mathias, Ji Won Park, and Oliver Stolpe

Public Office, Private Interests: Accountability through Income and Asset Disclosure (2012)

On the Take: Criminalizing Illicit Enrichment to Fight Corruption (2012) by Lindy Muzila, Michelle Morales, Marianne Mathias, and Tammar Berger

The Puppet Masters: How the Corrupt Use Legal Structures to Hide Stolen Assets and What to Do about It (2011) by Emile van der Does de Willebois, J. C. Sharman, Robert Harrison, Ji Won Park, and Emily Halter

Barriers to Asset Recovery: An Analysis of the Key Barriers and Recommendations for Action (2011) by Kevin Stephenson, Larissa Gray, and Ric Power

Asset Recovery Handbook: A Guide for Practitioners (2011) by Jean-Pierre Brun, Larissa Gray, Clive Scott, and Kevin Stephenson

Politically Exposed Persons: Preventive Measures for the Banking Sector (2010) by Theodore S. Greenberg, Larissa Gray, Delphine Schantz, Carolin Gardner, and Michael Latham

Stolen Asset Recovery: A Good Practices Guide for Non-conviction Based Asset Forfeiture (2009) by Theodore S. Greenberg, Linda M. Samuel, Wingate Grant, and Larissa Gray

All books in the StAR Series are available for free at
https://openknowledge.worldbank.org/handle/10986/2172

Stolen Asset Recovery Initiative Series

Taxing Crime

A Whole-of-Government Approach to Fighting Corruption, Money Laundering, and Tax Crimes

Jean-Pierre Brun
Ana Cebreiro Gomez
Rita Julien
Joy Waruguru Ndubai
Jeffrey Owens
Siddhesh Rao
Yara Esquivel Soto

WORLD BANK GROUP

Contents

Foreword

The international community continues to face perennial challenges, whether in the form of a global pandemic, the ongoing threat of climate change, or the threat of armed conflicts on a scale not seen since World War II. In this context, maintaining trust in public institutions and safeguarding public resources are imperative to enable effective policy responses. The fight against corruption and tax evasion remains at the heart of this mission.

Corruption in its different forms has plagued most countries, albeit to different degrees, harming vulnerable populations and eroding the funding for much-needed public services and investment. Tax evasion and other crimes are just as pernicious. Although the international community has placed fighting corruption and tax evasion at the top of the global agenda, the means used to perpetrate and profit from financial crimes—whether in the form of corruption, tax evasion, or money laundering—are ever evolving, adapting to policy, regulatory, and enforcement trends and exploiting weaknesses within systems and across jurisdictions. The release of the Pandora Papers in October 2021, and more recently the challenges encountered in implementing financial sanctions, is a stark reminder that opaque offshore structures are still widely available to those who wish to obfuscate beneficial ownership and conceal the illegal provenance of their wealth.

Policy makers must think creatively to make their systems more agile and able to respond promptly and effectively to persistent and emerging risks linked to the proceeds of crime. Exploring synergies among ongoing efforts to tackle corruption, tax evasion, and money laundering by different domestic agencies and across borders is a key component of this response. Identifying and recognizing the value of the information available to government agencies and ensuring that this information is appropriately shared among them as well as with foreign counterparts would undoubtedly unlock significant gains in detecting, investigating, and prosecuting financial crimes.

This is the primary objective of this study, which was born out of the World Bank's commitment to tackle illicit financial flows to promote resilient, inclusive development. It is the product of fruitful cooperation between the World Bank–United Nations Office on Drugs and Crime (UNODC) Stolen Asset Recovery Initiative (StAR) and the Global Tax Policy Center at the Institute for Austrian and International Tax Law, WU (Vienna University of Economics and Business).

By providing stakeholders with effective tools to design policies for inter-agency and international cooperation, this study will contribute to the fight against illicit financial flows and thus to the mobilization of resources that are essential to economic development.

Mark Pieth
President of the Board
Basel Institute on Governance

Acknowledgments

Taxing Crime: A Whole-of-Government Approach to Fighting Corruption, Money Laundering, and Tax Crimes was authored by a team composed of experts from the World Bank–United Nations Office on Drugs and Crime (UNODC) Stolen Asset Recovery Initiative (StAR) and the Global Tax Policy Center at the Institute for Austrian and International Tax Law, WU (Vienna University of Economics and Business). The team was led by Jean-Pierre Brun (World Bank, StAR) and composed of Ana Cebreiro Gomez and Yara Esquivel Soto (World Bank) and Rita Julien, Joy Waruguru Ndubai, Jeffrey Owens, and Siddhesh Rao (Global Tax Policy Center).

The authors would like to thank peer reviewers Thabo Legwaila (Office of Tax Ombudsman, South Africa), Rick McDonell (former executive secretary, Financial Action Task Force), Nilimesh Baruah (Organisation for Economic Co-operation and Development), James Brumby (senior adviser, Governance Global Practice, World Bank), Amir Shaikh (adviser to the senior vice president and general counsel, World Bank), and Philippe de Meneval (lead private sector specialist, World Bank) for their thoughtful and constructive comments.

The authors are also thankful for the input provided by experts who reviewed the draft text, some of whom participated in the virtual practitioners' workshop held in April 2021. They brought their invaluable experience in conducting criminal and tax investigations, asset tracing, international cooperation, and related legal actions. Their input is reflected in the appendix of cases as practical illustrations of cooperation, and it also helped refine the analysis and recommendations in the study to account for the specific challenges to and opportunities for cooperation encountered in practice. The participating experts were Edward Karanja (Kenya), Paul Keyton (Mauritius), Xolisile Khanyile (South Africa), Brett Martin (Australia), Emil Meddy (Ghana), Sophie Meingast (UNODC), Cristina Muengo (Angola), Muhammad Nami (Nigeria), David Palmer (World Bank), Preya Raghoonundun (Mauritius), David Ross (Australia), Nisrine Roudies (Tunisia), Salvatore Russo (Italy), Fred Salimane (South Africa), Michael Tukei (Uganda), and Lize van Shoor (Zambia).

Finally, the authors would like to thank Lei Shi (intern, Georgetown Law School) for collecting the relevant cases; Yasmin De Magalhaes Pinto Almeida (young professional, World Bank) for her assistance in finalizing the peer-reviewed version; Emile van der Does de Willebois (lead financial sector specialist, Financial Stability and Integrity team, World Bank) for his support and guidance throughout the process; as well as Cedric Mousset (practice manager, World Bank) and Jean Pesme (global director, World Bank) for their active support of the study.

StAR Stolen Asset Recovery Initiative
The World Bank • UNODC

TAX
Institute for Austrian and
International Tax Law **Vienna**
WU Global Tax Policy Center

About the Authors

Jean-Pierre Brun is a senior financial specialist at the World Bank, specializing in anti-money laundering policies, technical assistance, and stolen asset recovery in the context of the Stolen Asset Recovery Initiative (StAR). He is the lead author of five books (*Asset Recovery Handbook* (two editions); *Going for Broke; Public Wrongs, Private Actions; Identification and Quantification of the Proceeds of Bribery;* and *Barriers to Asset Recovery*). Brun recently led the design of the Board-approved World Bank Strategy against Illicit Financial Flows. He has also designed and delivered a training curriculum for investigators and prosecutors in numerous countries. Previously, in France, he served as a prosecutor and investigating judge specializing in white-collar crime, as a chief auditor at the French government's Auditing Court, and as a director for Deloitte in Paris. He holds a master's degree in political science from the Paris Institute of Political Studies (Sciences Po), a master's degree in criminal law, and a certification to practice as a prosecutor or judge from the French National School for Judicial Studies.

Ana Cebreiro Gomez is a senior economist on the Global Tax Team at the World Bank. She leads the international tax work at the global level, including the tax transparency agenda and its link with illicit financial flows. Since joining the World Bank in 2013, she has been implementing technical assistance tax projects and supporting lending operations covering both tax policy and administration. Cebreiro Gomez has more than 25 years of expertise in the tax area. Before joining the World Bank, she worked for nine years at the Centre for Tax Policy and Administration at the Organisation for Economic Co-operation and Development (OECD) in Paris. Previously, she held positions as an economic consultant at DotEcon Economic Consulting and as a research economist for Her Majesty's Revenue and Customs agency in London. She holds master's and doctorate degrees in economics from the University of Essex in the United Kingdom and a master's degree in applied public economics from Universidad Autonoma de Barcelona.

Rita Julien teaches in the International Tax Law LLM program at Vienna University of Economics and Business (WU) and conducts research for the focus group on unexplained wealth in the Tax Transparency and Corruption Project at the university's Global Tax Policy Center. She will soon join New York

University School of Law as a visiting assistant professor of tax law. Previously, she was a graduate tax scholar in the LLM program at Georgetown Law. She holds a doctoral degree in business law from WU, where she worked as a research and teaching associate at the Institute for Austrian and International Tax Law, and an LLM with a specialization in European and international tax law from the University of Luxembourg.

Joy Waruguru Ndubai is a teaching and research associate and a doctoral candidate at the Global Tax Policy Center at the Institute for Austrian and International Tax Law, WU (Vienna University of Economics and Business). Previously, she worked as global tax adviser at ActionAid Denmark, with Oxfam GB (Kenya office) and the Tax Justice Network Africa, and as a tax adviser at KPMG East Africa. She holds an LLM in taxation from the London School of Economics and Political Sciences and an LLB from SOAS University of London. She is currently pursuing a doctorate in business law with a focus on special economic zones and their regulation in international trade, investment, and tax law.

Jeffrey Owens is director of the Global Tax Policy Center at the Institute for Austrian and International Tax Law, WU (Vienna University of Economics and Business). He also serves as a senior policy adviser to the global vice chair of tax at EY (Ernst & Young) and as a senior adviser to the United Nations Tax Committee, the Inter-American Development Bank, the United Nations Conference on Trade and Development, and a number of regional tax administration organizations. He led tax work at the OECD for more than 20 years. He holds a doctorate degree in economics from the University of Cambridge.

Siddhesh Rao is a doctoral candidate at the Global Tax Policy Center at the Institute for Austrian and International Tax Law, WU (Vienna University of Economics and Business). His research focuses on policy issues of money laundering, illicit financial flows, taxes, and good governance. Previously, Rao worked in a private tax practice in India advising multinational enterprises and corporations He is a member of the Institute of Chartered Accountants of India and holds an LLM in international tax law from WU.

Yara Esquivel Soto is a senior financial sector specialist in the World Bank's Financial Stability and Integrity Global Unit. She is an attorney with 20 years of experience in investigating fraud and corruption. She works on anti-money laundering, terrorism financing, and asset recovery in Latin America and Africa, and led the World Bank's first work on illicit flows—the effects of the cocaine trade on the economy of Colombia. Previously, she served as an anticorruption prosecutor in her native Costa Rica, where she investigated a former head of state, and as a fraud and corruption investigator for the United Nations in Africa and the World Bank in Latin America. She holds a master's degree in international human rights law from Oxford University.

Executive Summary

Preventing, detecting, and recovering the illicit financial flows derived from tax evasion, corruption, and money laundering are a global development priority. Although the magnitude of illicit financial flows is a matter of debate, their important implications for economies are widely recognized. Tax evasion and corruption drain limited public resources, and often they hurt the most vulnerable populations by depleting the funds for much-needed services. Beyond the budget, tax evasion and corruption harm the social fabric by fueling inequality and eroding trust in public institutions and the rule of law. Illicit financial flows are then a major obstacle to resilient, inclusive development.

The similarities and interconnectedness of these crimes suggest that huge benefits would accrue from enhancing interagency cooperation and exploring synergies. Indeed, these crimes are often connected. The proceeds generated by corruption are regularly underdeclared and undertaxed, adding a tax crime component to the corrupt conduct. At the same time, tax evasion schemes can hide further forms of criminality. For example, tax deductions for payments of false invoices can be a front for bribe payments and a way to transfer and launder ill-gotten gains. Moreover, corruption, money laundering, and tax evasion are often enabled by the use of similar opaque corporate structures and arrangements to conceal ultimate beneficial ownership. In the end, those committing these crimes rely on inconsistent and, at times, poor interagency and international cooperation to evade detection and prosecution.

Despite their strong connections, these financial crimes have often been pursued by agencies working in silos, limiting the potential for more effective detection and prosecution. Each category of crime frequently falls within the mandates of specialized agencies—tax authorities, financial intelligence units (FIUs), anticorruption agencies, and other investigative bodies.[1] When agencies have access to different types and sources of information and they analyze data through the prism of their individual mandates, they often miss red flags indicative of financial crimes or information relevant to the mandates of other agencies.

Moreover, large-scale financial crimes often involve financial flows across borders, raising the need for international cooperation. This international dimension calls for an additional layer of cooperation to exchange information, obtain evidence, and ultimately enforce confiscation, as well as the provisional measures needed to detect and recover the proceeds of these crimes.

Interagency cooperation has an important strategic role to play, not only in the context of investigations, but also at the prosecution stage. Relying on interagency teams to investigate and prosecute financial crimes avoids potential duplication of efforts, especially where more than one agency is empowered to prosecute the same type of offense. It also enhances investigative and prosecutorial capacity by bringing together different types of expertise and enabling access to the unique procedures available to each agency. Cooperation between tax authorities and law enforcement agencies (LEAs) at the prosecution stage may also allow simultaneous prosecution via the national courts and specialized tax tribunals, thereby increasing the chances of success. Such cooperation could limit a suspect's ability to evade prosecution and increase the likelihood of recovery of at least some of the assets.

Clearly, then, a "whole-of-government" approach is needed to enable agencies to successfully detect, prosecute, and recover the proceeds of interconnected financial crimes. This approach requires commitment, investment, and coordination at various levels of government to overcome existing barriers.

Specific steps toward a policy promoting this whole-of-government approach might be the following:

- Enhanced cooperation and information sharing among agencies should be a policy objective. To help them identify any overlap, interdependencies, and opportunities for closer coordination, policy makers could map out the mandates of the relevant agencies, such as tax authorities and law enforcement agencies, and the types and sources of information available to each. A strong public policy stance on interagency cooperation is vital to overcoming legal, operational, and cultural barriers and can facilitate the needed legislative changes.

- An appropriate legal framework free from unreasonable and disproportionate legal barriers to the exchange of information will ensure successful interagency cooperation. The legal and regulatory frameworks governing the agencies—and, in particular, governing the powers, duties, and procedures for interagency cooperation—need to be clear, aligned, and easy to implement. Expanding the scope and definition of tax crimes to include them as predicate offenses to money laundering in line with the Financial Action Task Force (FATF) standards is a prerequisite for linking the work of tax authorities and FIUs.

- At the operational level, technical and structural elements must be in place to overcome challenges and ensure that information flows smoothly in a timely, cost-efficient way. Countries should design and implement effective internal policies and procedures governing interagency cooperation by, for example, adopting written cooperation agreements and issuing guidance for other agencies on how to request information. Agencies should also develop the technological capabilities needed to share sensitive and potentially large volumes of data, while securing the confidentiality of the information. Meanwhile, two preconditions must be fulfilled to secure effective cooperation: (1) adequate financial and human resources must be made available to the relevant agencies, and (2) staff integrity must be secured through selection and management processes. At the same time, taking steps to prevent abuse of power and misuse of data is essential.

- Cultural barriers commonly exist within and across agencies. These may include a lack of trust and understanding among officials, insufficient communication, and other practices that delay or impede cooperation. Incentivizing agencies to exchange knowledge at the staff level, such as via staff secondments or joint training sessions, would help build trust among agencies and encourage the use of informal channels of cooperation, which are a key component of effective interagency cooperation.

In addition, to achieve enhanced interagency and international exchange of operational information in the context of corruption, money laundering, and tax crime cases, this study puts forth the following recommendations:

- Overcome the legal barriers to information exchange. At the domestic level, the legislative framework should formally acknowledge the link between tax crimes and broader financial crimes, authorize or mandate tax authorities and LEAs to disclose information whenever there are reasonable grounds to do so, and set up internal standard operating procedures governing interagency exchange of information. At the international level, removing the legal and administrative barriers to international cooperation between the relevant agencies and tax authorities and FIUs of counterpart countries is crucial.

- Enhance the availability and collection of pertinent information by enacting legal provisions to recover unexplained wealth, illicit enrichment, or unjustified resources. Tax forms should include questions for politically exposed persons, and mandatory disclosure rules and beneficial ownership frameworks should be adopted.

- Overcome operational barriers to the exchange of information. At the domestic level, effectiveness requires adopting formal models for cooperation between agencies, providing the relevant training, establishing secured systems of communications and exchange of information, supporting informal channels of cooperation, and establishing joint task forces in dealing with recurring or larger crimes. At the international level, conducting international investigations through fully integrated and coordinated interagency mechanisms should maximize the use of both informal and formal processes for exchange of law enforcement and tax information.

- Overcome cultural and political barriers by both balancing efforts to exchange information with confidentiality, privacy, and data protection to promote trust and cultural buy-in and using all international instruments in international corruption, money laundering, and tax crime investigations.

Policy makers could also consider taking steps beyond these recommendations. One example is introducing laws to expand information-gathering possibilities, including those related to mandatory disclosure of the use of aggressive tax avoidance schemes. Another is adopting unexplained wealth or illicit enrichment laws that could provide authorities with the power to query a person's income or wealth that has no known legitimate sources, but within a sound legal regime and robust good governance framework.

Note

1. In this report, the term *law enforcement agencies* (LEAs) refers to investigative agencies, anticorruption agencies, and FIUs, unless otherwise specified.

Abbreviations

AEOI	automatic exchange of information
AML	anti-money laundering
ARIN	asset recovery interagency network
BEPS	base erosion and profit shifting
CAA	Competent Authority Agreement
CARIN	Camden Asset Recovery Inter-agency Network
CFT	countering the financing of terrorism
CIOT	Chartered Institute of Taxation
CRS MCAA	Common Reporting Standards Multilateral Competent Authority Agreement
CSO	civil society organization
CTR	currency transaction report
CTS	common transmission system
EOIR	Exchange of Information on Request
EU	European Union
FACTI	The High-Level Panel on International Financial Accountability, Transparency and Integrity for Achieving the 2030 Agenda
FATF	Financial Action Task Force
FIU	financial intelligence unit
ICIJ	International Consortium of Investigative Journalists
IFF	illicit financial flow
JIT	joint investigative team
LEA	law enforcement agency
MCMA	Multilateral Convention on Mutual Administrative Assistance in Tax Matters
MDR	mandatory disclosure rule
MLA	mutual legal assistance
MLAT	mutual legal assistance treaty
MoU	memorandum of understanding
MTC	Model Tax Convention
OECD	Organisation for Economic Co-operation and Development
PEP	politically exposed person
SAR	suspicious activity report
SLA	service-level agreement

StAR	Stolen Asset Recovery Initiative
STR	suspicious transaction report
TIEA	tax information exchange agreement
UN	United Nations
UNCAC	United Nations Convention against Corruption
UNCTAD	United Nations Conference on Trade and Development
UNODC	United Nations Office on Drugs and Crime
UNTOC/Palermo Convention	United Nations Convention Against Transnational Organized Crime
UWO	unexplained wealth order
VAT	value added tax
WU	Vienna University of Economics and Business

All dollar amounts are US dollars unless otherwise indicated.

1. Introduction

1.1 Battling Crime and Corruption: A Priority

Fighting corruption, money laundering, and tax crimes, as well as recovering the proceeds of crime, are now a high priority for the international community. Reports recently issued by the United Nations Conference on Trade and Development (UNCTAD), the High-Level Panel on International Financial Accountability, Transparency and Integrity for Achieving the 2030 Agenda (FACTI Panel), and other organizations highlight the challenges that tax and other financial crimes continue to pose for national economic development and stability. They rob developing countries of scarce and much-needed revenue and the broader global financial system of stability by undermining the integrity of cross-border financial flows (UNCTAD 2020; UNCTAD and UNODC 2020; UN FACTI 2021). Illicit financial flows (IFFs) and theft of assets are a barrier to financing sustainable development, especially for developing countries facing financial constraints and greater pressure to mobilize their domestic resources.

The battle against corruption, money laundering, and tax crimes is complex and requires tenacity and creativity. It often involves close coordination and collaboration between domestic agencies and ministries in multiple jurisdictions with different legal systems and procedures. In this context, making full use of the cooperation between tax authorities and law enforcement agencies (LEAs) at the domestic and international levels is crucial. Meanwhile, certain preconditions are needed to enable information sharing between agencies, including ensuring the integrity of agents and building trust and open relationships.

To further promote the tools needed for this enhanced cooperation in the fight against corruption, money laundering, and tax crimes, the World Bank–United Nations Office on Drugs and Crime (UNODC) Stolen Asset Recovery Initiative (StAR) and the Global Tax Policy Center at the Institute for Austrian and International Tax Law, WU (Vienna University of Economics and Business), jointly prepared this publication.

1.2 Objectives

Many criminal activities, including corruption, money laundering, and fraud, have a tax crime component, which consists of allowing individuals to benefit from undeclared and untaxed income or assets. At the same time, tax evasion schemes often involve corrupt or fraudulent conduct such as undervaluation, false accounting, fictitious invoicing, or bribery of public officials to look the other way. Because of the important links between various financial crimes and tax crimes identified at the national and international levels, country authorities should develop whole-of-government approaches to the pursuit of lawbreakers (UN FACTI 2021). These approaches would entail cooperation between a multitude of agencies, including anticorruption authorities, financial intelligence units (FIUs), financial regulators and supervisors, police, prosecutors, tax authorities, and customs authorities (OECD and World Bank 2018).

Tax authorities can be especially important allies in combating corruption, money laundering, and other financial crimes (OECD and World Bank 2018). In addition to examining the returns filed by taxpayers, tax authorities have access to the transactions and financial records of millions of individuals and entities (OECD 2013). However, tax authorities are not always aware of the typical indicators of corruption, money laundering, and other financial crimes not related to taxes. They also may not be sufficiently aware that they are responsible for sharing suspicious information with the appropriate law enforcement agencies, such as FIUs or police (OECD 2013). Questions also arise about whether sharing tax information with LEAs could affect the voluntary tax compliance by individuals and whether it could constitute a privacy violation.

Conversely, the information collected and investigations carried out by anticorruption agencies, FIUs, and other LEAs can reveal not only corruption and money laundering offenses, but also tax violations and crimes (FATF 2012a). Unfortunately, it is not uncommon for these entities to work in silos, disconnected from tax authorities and vice versa. Impediments to cooperation might be legal, operational, or cultural in nature.

Having agencies working in silos misses opportunities and creates inefficiencies. Because of the links between financial crimes, the sources of intelligence stemming from agencies with different mandates could, if combined, create a more complete picture of a given case, generate more actionable and accurate information, and ultimately result in greater efficiency in successfully carrying out these respective mandates. Countries are therefore dismantling the barriers impeding cooperation and information sharing in line with evolving international standards.[1]

For these reasons, cooperation should be encouraged all along the "value chain" of the law enforcement process—from initial intelligence gathering to investigating, prosecuting, and eventually recovering criminal proceeds—among agencies addressing different financial crimes. Cooperation should be "in accordance with domestic laws, policies and procedures," including the appropriate safeguards for data protection and confidentiality, and "should be results-driven, not process-driven" (Schlenther 2017, 86).

This report evaluates opportunities and emerging trends and tools that can foster more integrated interagency collaboration and bolster investigations and prosecutions of financial crimes, ranging from greater cooperation between tax authorities and LEAs to laws on "unexplained wealth," professional enablers (OECD 2021), and beneficial ownership registries. It is largely directed at senior policy makers. However, the analysis, case study documentation, and recommendations may also enable practitioners, advocacy groups, and professionals to develop a more in-depth understanding of the practices and benefits of inter-agency cooperation. It is hoped members of the judiciary will also read this report because they will be deciding on cases arising from interagency cooperation.

1.3 Methodology

This report was drafted jointly by the StAR Initiative and the Global Tax Policy Center, drawing on their respective areas of expertise. The report also draws on the work of the Tax and Good Governance project, a joint project undertaken by the World Bank, UNODC, and the Global Tax Policy Center.[2] It relies as well on examples of how tax audits and investigations can lead to uncovering white-collar crime (focusing on corruption offenses and money laundering) and how criminal investigations can, in turn, lead to prosecuting tax evasion or simply recovering unpaid taxes.

The first draft of this report was presented and discussed at a virtual prac-titioner workshop held in April 2021. Participants included tax auditors and investigators, law enforcement, financial investigators, investigating magis-trates, and prosecutors from developed and developing jurisdictions and from civil and common law systems. Bringing to the gathering their experience in conducting criminal and tax investigations, asset tracing, international cooperation, and related legal actions, they discussed how tax and criminal investigations can be integrated to both improve the effectiveness of each investigation and facilitate an exchange of information and access to interna-tional cooperation channels.

Input from practitioners explored real-life examples of interagency coopera-tion, specifically in corruption, money laundering, and tax evasion. This input is reflected not only in this report's appendix of case studies as practical illustra-tions of cooperation, but also in refinements of the analysis and recommenda-tions in this study to account for the specific challenges to and opportunities for cooperation encountered in practice.

The final version of the study was peer reviewed following World Bank pro-cedures. The resulting comments were discussed in a virtual decision meeting held on May 27, 2021, and chaired by Jean Pesme, global director of the Finance, Competitiveness and Innovation Global Practice at the World Bank.

1.4 How This Study Can Be Used

This study is designed to be a reference and an advocacy report for policy mak-ers, but it also contains information useful to practitioners, including law enforce-ment officials, investigating magistrates, and prosecutors. It is not designed to be a detailed compendium of the law, institutions, and practices needed to fight tax evasion and financial crime. Instead, it focuses on how to maximize interagency and international cooperation, how to use criminal law to help fight tax evasion, and, conversely, how tax investigations can be used in criminal investigations and prosecution of financial crimes.

The report identifies and highlights legal frameworks and practices that should be considered and developed to enhance cooperation between tax authorities and LEAs at the domestic and international levels, thereby building on synergies between investigations and prosecutions of corruption, money laundering, and tax crimes. It also identifies the existing gaps and provides practical recommendations for tax authorities and LEAs seeking to implement or refine their strategies to address tax evasion and other associated financial crimes effectively.

Nonetheless, implementation of interagency cooperation should be monitored carefully over time. The credible threat of prosecution is important to dissuade and deter crimes. If prosecutions do not result in successful convictions, the credibility of the institutions involved could be affected. Depending on the circumstances, it may be necessary to introduce stronger civil regimes to complement criminal regimes.

Finally, the effectiveness of the relevant agencies depends on the availability of adequate human and technical resources and on staff integrity. Moreover, in some jurisdictions, increased use of tax and law enforcement may be abused for political purposes.

Meanwhile, this study is not intended to deal in detail with the preconditions and the factors critical to success. It is rather a contribution to an ongoing program conducted in East Africa and Asia by the World Bank to support the fight against tax evasion and money laundering. Other key elements of this program are specific risk assessments centered on a comprehensive approach to illicit financial flows, training, and assistance in drafting the relevant legal and supervisory frameworks and addressing the preconditions of effectiveness.

The main recommendations in this report will be discussed at national and regional meetings organized in the context of the World Bank's overarching program on countering IFFs and the Global Tax Policy Center's program on tax and good governance in Africa.

1.5 Structure of the Study

The study is organized around the key axes of analysis that help sort out the various points at which action can be taken. It considers the legal elements versus the operational elements of cooperation at the domestic and international levels and throughout the major stages of the enforcement process—investigation, prosecution, and recovery.

Chapter 2 presents a host of strategic considerations for establishing channels between tax and criminal investigative agencies to exchange information. Chapter 3 explains how to develop approaches combining tax and financial crime prosecution as part of an interagency asset recovery strategy. Chapter 4 then deals with approaches to developing interagency exchanges of information at the regional and international levels. Finally, the concluding chapter 5 provides recommendations for future efforts to improve interagency cooperation and enhance the role of tax authorities in supporting efforts to combat money laundering and corruption, and vice versa.

Two helpful features are included as well. The appendix contains case studies illustrating effective interagency cooperation, including at the international level. It is followed by a glossary that defines many of the specialized terms used in the study. Because jurisdictions often use different terms to describe the same legal concept or procedure, the glossary provides examples of alternative terms.

Notes

1. On the anti-money laundering (AML) side, in the 2012 revision of its recommendations the Financial Action Task Force (FATF) added tax crime as a predicate to money laundering and added tax authorities as "competent authorities" throughout the recommendations. On the tax side, in 2014, the Global Forum on Transparency and Exchange of Information for Tax Purposes adopted the FATF definition of beneficial ownership and thus aligned its standards with the AML standard on beneficial ownership (see FATF 2012b).
2. The Institute for Austrian and International Tax Law is within the Vienna University of Economics and Business. The Tax and Good Governance project (2015–18) identified the links between corruption, money laundering, and tax crimes and preceded the current project on Tax Transparency and Corruption (2019–23). For more information, see https://www.wu .ac.at/taxlaw/institute/gtpc/current-projects/tax-and-good-governance.

References

FATF (Financial Action Task Force). 2012a. *Operational Issues: Financial Investigations Guidance*. Paris: FATF. http://www.fatf-gafi.org/media/fatf/documents/reports/Operational %20Issues_Financial%20investigations%20Guidance.pdf.

FATF (Financial Action Task Force). 2012b. *The FATF Recommendations*. Paris: FATF. https://www.fatf-gafi.org/media/fatf/documents/recommendations/pdfs/FATF%20 Recommendations%202012.pdf.

OECD (Organisation for Economic Co-operation and Development). 2013. "The Role of Tax Examiners and Tax Auditors." In *Bribery and Corruption Awareness Handbook for Tax Examiners and Tax Auditors*, 15–18. https://www.oecd-ilibrary.org/docserver/9789264 205376-5-en.pdf?expires=1583685923&id=id&accname=guest&checksum=E3DC0539 22746958894C20B18F5AA90B.

OECD (Organisation for Economic Co-operation and Development). 2021. *Ending the Shell Game: Cracking Down on the Professionals Who Enable Tax and White Collar Crimes*. Paris: OECD Publishing.

OECD (Organisation for Economic Co-operation and Development) and World Bank. 2018. *Improving Co-operation between Tax Authorities and Anti-Corruption Authorities in Combating Tax Crime and Corruption*. Paris: OECD Publishing.

Schlenther, Bernd. 2017. "Tax Administrations, Financial Intelligence Units, Law Enforcement Agencies: How to Work Together?" In *Inter-agency Cooperation and Good Tax Governance in Africa*, edited by Jeffrey Owens, Rick McDonell, Riël Franzsen, and Jude Amos. Pretoria, South Africa: Pretoria University Law Press.

UNCTAD (United Nations Conference on Trade and Development). 2020. *Tackling Illicit Financial Flows for Sustainable Development in Africa*. Geneva: UNCTAD. https://unctad.org/system/files/official-document/aldcafrica2020_en.pdf.

UNCTAD (United Nations Conference on Trade and Development) and UNODC (United Nations Office on Drugs and Crime). 2020. *Conceptual Framework for the Statistical Measurement of Illicit Financial Flows*. Geneva and Vienna: UNCTAD and UNODC. https://www.unodc.org/unodc/en/data-and-analysis/iff.html.

UN FACTI Panel (United Nations Financial Accountability, Transparency and Integrity Panel). 2021. *Financial Integrity for Sustainable Development: Report of the High Level Panel on International Financial Accountability, Transparency and Integrity for Achieving the 2030 Agenda*. New York: United Nations.

2. Establishing Exchange of Information Channels for Tax and Criminal Investigative Agencies

2.1 Introduction

A whole-of-government approach to fighting financial and tax crime entails cooperation among a multitude of agencies, including anticorruption authorities, financial intelligence units (FIUs), financial regulators and supervisors, police, prosecutors, exchange control departments, tax authorities, and customs authorities. The approach requires recognizing the value of information held by each agency, fulfilling the preconditions of information sharing, establishing an appropriate legal framework, and addressing the operational challenges to implementing the framework.

2.2 Recognizing the Types and Value of Information Held by Different Agencies

Because of the strong link between tax crimes and other financial crimes, organizing a framework that encourages, authorizes, or mandates tax authorities to share with law enforcement agencies (LEAs) certain information, and vice versa, is vital. Tax authorities routinely conduct tax audits to verify that taxpayers are meeting their obligations and paying what they owe. During these audits, the authorities have access to information on assets and financial transactions that can be used by LEAs to launch criminal investigations not only into tax fraud, but also into corruption, bribery, embezzlement, and money laundering.

Tax authorities also collect data from third parties such as banks, other financial institutions, share registries, and superannuation funds, as well as information from local government agencies and statutory authorities that they use to uncover anomalies, which can also be helpful to LEAs.

Data collected by or available to tax authorities generally are from a variety of sources, including:

- Tax registration information and filed tax returns
- Accounting books and records of businesses
- Periodic (quarterly, annual, transaction-based) returns from businesses
- Customs declarations
- Whistleblower complaints or tax evasion petitions
- Exchange of information with foreign governments
- Information supplied by other jurisdictions via automatic, spontaneous, or upon-request routes
- Reports from commissions of inquiry and research reports

Box 2.1 lists examples of information that may help investigators identify suspicious transactions and criminal activity.

BOX 2.1	Legal, Financial, and Other Relevant Information Often Uncovered by Tax Authorities

The following information may emerge from tax authorities:

- Beneficial ownership, which could determine the connection between a natural person and an asset, financial account/transaction, legal person, or legal arrangement

- Assets disproportionate to declared or known sources of income

- Accretion of wealth by politically exposed persons or close relatives (for example, acquisition of high-value real property)

- Receipt of abnormal or sudden profits from commodity and stock markets, substantial exempt incomes (such as agricultural income), or other unidentifiable sources of income

- Receipt of abnormal or frequent gifts from unrelated persons

- Spending beyond one's declared income and assets

- Family members or associates of politically exposed persons controlling shell companies, trusts, or holdings that, in turn, hold valuable assets

- Instances of nondeclaration of a conflict of interest discovered in tax audits

- Fictitious, overpriced, or underpriced invoices uncovered in tax audits that may be used to disguise illicit payments, notably to businesses controlled by corrupt public officials or their associates or family members

- Unusual monetary deposits from foreign banks that may not be captured by anti-money laundering reporting requirements for transactions conducted through off-system channels

One of the most common forms of public corruption is bribery—that is, receipt of an undue advantage in return for the performance or nonperformance of an official act or duty.[1] A company that pays a bribe to a government official will not record it as such[2] in its accounting books and records. In practice, bribes are typically concealed, paid out, and recorded as some admissible expense.[3] The discovery by tax authorities of questionable payments can thus trigger suspicions that they are only recorded to offset the value of inappropriate transactions made with corrupt intent. Where a framework to cooperate with the relevant LEA is available, timely disclosure of questionable payments by the tax authority can trigger the launch of corruption investigations.

Cooperation can be particularly effective because tax authorities often have essential skills and tools for detecting unreported or unexplained taxable income and wealth or deductible expenses that cannot be proven. These skills and tools place tax authorities in a unique position to identify potentially illicit income or wealth derived from the proceeds of other nontax crimes[4] and illicit payments disguised as deductible expenses. Although tax authorities are unlikely to uncover the true nature of potentially illicit funds, if allowed to share their findings with the appropriate law enforcement agency, the latter can take the investigation forward. For example, a payment made to a service provider without evidence of services actually rendered cannot be used as a deductible business expense, which falls within the tax authorities' purview, but it may be an indicator of potential money laundering, which could be further investigated by the appropriate LEA.

Conversely, information collected by other agencies can assist tax authorities. FIUs receive suspicious transaction reports (STRs) and suspicious activity reports (SARs) from reporting institutions, which include financial institutions and designated categories of nonfinancial businesses and professions such as lawyers, accountants, real estate agents, dealers in precious metals and stones, casinos, and trust and company service providers (FATF 2012a).[5] STRs can be particularly useful to tax authorities because they can provide insight into an individual or entity's private transactions, which, in turn, can complement the tax authorities' assessment of their risk profile for noncompliance (OECD 2015a). STRs have proven useful to tax authorities in practice, according to countries surveyed (see cases 1 and 2 in the appendix for an illustration). For example, according to the National Crime Agency (NCA) in the United Kingdom, which acts as the country's FIU, Her Majesty's Revenue and Customs (HMRC) agency "indicates that around a fifth of STRs received identify a new subject of interest and a quarter lead to new enquiries in relation to direct taxation matters."[6]

Currency transaction reports (CTRs), issued when cash beyond a prescribed threshold is paid or received, are also a possible source of meaningful information. A monitoring mechanism applied to financial institutions, CTRs may arise when a transaction or a series of aggregated transactions exceed a prescribed amount. This amount varies by country, and financial institutions must submit this report to the FIU within a specified period (usually immediately or within 24 hours). In developing or transitioning economies, many businesses operate in the informal economy and so are not registered for tax purposes. By sharing the relevant CTRs with tax authorities, financial institutions enable those authorities to more easily identify businesses operating in the informal economy and bring them into the tax framework.

Anticorruption investigators may also come across information that would be useful to tax authorities as strong indicators of potential accompanying tax crimes. Although anticorruption investigators routinely investigate suspicious assets or transactions involving public officials, family members, or their associates that are not consistent with their known income, such potential corruption often also has a tax component. Indeed, assets and transactions concealed to obfuscate their illicit source or purpose (and posing a tax liability) are also unlikely to be declared to the tax authorities.

Anticorruption investigations may even uncover hidden accounts or "parallel" accounting records used by companies to operate slush funds, which can reveal an array of funds and transactions unlikely to have been declared for tax purposes. For example, investigations into bribes paid by a company through offshore accounts may also uncover the use of those accounts to make other concealed payments, such as undeclared bonuses to executives. One benefit of sharing such information with the tax authorities is that in cases in which all elements required to prove a corruption offense cannot be met and the corruption charge is unlikely to succeed, the government may at least succeed in reclaiming overdue unpaid taxes on the transactions or funds, along with interest and penalties (OECD and World Bank 2018).

Moreover, when LEAs use special investigative measures such as searches and electronic and telephone interceptions (wiretapping), they may uncover evidence of crimes, including tax crimes, tax administrative violations, or even relationships that may be relevant to determining the effective control of an entity or account. In addition to enabling LEAs to identify possible corruption and facilitators who often have criminal assets in their name, this information can be very useful to tax authorities.

2.3 Preconditions for Information Sharing: Overcoming Legal, Operational, and Cultural Barriers

Demonstrating the practical relevance and the added value of cooperation at each stage of pursuit of crime (including investigation, prosecution, and recovery) is a crucial prerequisite to overcoming commonly cited legal, operational, and cultural barriers and establishing more effective interagency cooperation (OECD and World Bank 2018). To do so, it is useful to map out the mandate of the agencies concerned (such as tax authorities, FIUs, and LEAs) and the types of information the agencies collect (Schlenther 2017). From this, it is possible to identify the overlaps and interdependencies between agencies (Schlenther 2017), making it clearer how much more effectively each agency could carry out its mandate through more seamless interagency cooperation, including from a cost perspective.

This exercise also helps agencies identify operational barriers—that is, practical or structural elements that create unnecessary or disproportionate friction in interagency information exchange—and address them. Addressing operational barriers can include designing operational procedures such as memoranda of understanding (MoUs) to underpin interagency cooperation where there are none, or improving and streamlining existing internal procedures where these are overly complex and lengthy. Other common operational barriers are gaps in agencies' technological abilities to share information involving sensitive or large volumes of data. In this case, developing joint technical solutions and platforms and training staff on how to use these solutions will be essential to ensuring a fluid exchange of information.

The security and confidentiality of sensitive tax and investigative information or intelligence are paramount for both legal and operational reasons, including to maintain public trust in institutions, particularly tax authorities. In this respect, it may be useful to look at the European Union (EU) directive on the protection of personal data and the way it has been implemented because it balances the need to investigate and prosecute criminal offenses with ensuring adequate protections for natural persons. In Article 37, transfer of personal data to a third country is conditioned on the presence of appropriate safeguards in the recipient country on protection of the personal data.[7] But the level of trust between people working together operationally, both in terms of sharing information and in task force investigations, is also crucial. For example, when confidential and sensitive information gathered in the context of a multiagency investigation is leaked to the press, cooperation and exchange of information can suffer as a result.

Information sharing between tax authorities and LEAs depends on the collaborative attitude of the concerned agencies. Raising awareness among tax authorities of the advantages of such a collaborative attitude and culture is vital. If tax authorities are only required or encouraged to ensure that business receipts or expenses are properly accounted for in the calculation of tax liabilities, they may not question whether the lack of plausibility or veracity of a certain expense is a sign of other criminal activities. For example, a fictitious payment to a consultancy controlled by an official identified by a tax authority is taxed as revenue for the consultancy. In addition, the payment is taxed at the level of the bribe payer because it is not accepted as a tax-deductible expense (reducing the taxable income) without proof of legitimate services provided. As a result, the tax bill for both the fake consultancy and the bribe payer goes up. If the tax authority considers its objective to be solely the assessment of tax liabilities, the tax authority will not dig deeper. However, if fighting corruption and other illicit financial activities is a government priority—that is, it is everyone's responsibility—then the tax authority will be more inclined to ask further questions.

Therefore, in many countries, tax authorities should at least be encouraged not only to identify, report, and investigate tax avoidance, but also to refer cases where the tax violations appear to be a warning sign of other criminal offenses, including corruption, bribery, embezzlement, and money laundering.[8] Although ensuring tax compliance will obviously remain the primary goal of tax officials, it is imperative that they also share a responsibility for fighting crimes more broadly. This objective is generally pursued by establishing a legislative mandate to report suspicious cases to the appropriate LEAs. Both the legislation and the guidance provided to tax authorities should require more diligence on their part.

To overcome legal barriers and to generate the political will required to enact legislative change, it is necessary to raise the awareness of policy makers and legislators about the gains such an expansion of mandates will produce. It is a good practice to enact special legislation mandating or authorizing information sharing to avoid uncertainties about and challenges to the legitimacy of criminal investigations based on transmissions from tax authorities (a topic explored later in this chapter).

Ensuring the integrity of all agents involved is another important precondition. This report does not go into detail about the mechanisms needed to ensure the integrity of agents, but, without a doubt, the relevant agencies must be staffed with professionals having the utmost integrity and competence.

2.4 Legal Frameworks for Cooperation at the Domestic Level

A building block for successful interagency cooperation is an appropriate legal framework. In this context, creating the overall framework for information sharing as well as specific provisions for beneficial ownership are essential to ensuring effective cooperation.

2.4.1 Creating the Legal Conditions for Information Sharing

First and foremost, domestic laws must enable information sharing between agencies in the same jurisdiction.[9] Beyond exchanging information, it is also worthwhile to consider laws that better enable information *gathering*, such as the inclusion of tax crimes as predicate offenses to money laundering, mandatory disclosure rules (OECD 2015b), and legislation targeting unexplained wealth orders (UWOs)[10] and whistleblower protection. Many such laws are now more widespread, and some even are accepted as best practice.

2.4.1.1 LAWS ENABLING INTERAGENCY INFORMATION SHARING
As global recognition of the links between tax crimes and other financial crimes has increased, efforts to implement laws that enable the relevant government agencies to share information have also accelerated (OECD and World Bank 2018). The inclusion of tax crimes as predicate offenses to money laundering

places an obligation on FIUs and LEAs to better understand the nature of these crimes and to cooperate more closely with tax authorities, including to improve their ability to identify potential corruption or money laundering. At the same time, the recognition of these links raises the need for engagement and exchange of information by LEAs and tax authorities.

Explicit Prohibitions on Information Sharing

In 2017, the OECD's review of 51 jurisdictions found that most countries provided gateways enabling police and public prosecutors to share information with tax authorities, or for direct access by tax authorities (OECD 2017a). On the other hand, countries do not always allow information held by an FIU to be shared with tax authorities. Although the OECD found that seven countries provided direct access and 41 others provided for some form of information sharing, some countries prohibited the FIU from sharing information with tax authorities investigating tax offenses (OECD 2017a).

A 2018 review by the OECD of cooperation between tax and anticorruption authorities found that in only two of 67 countries were tax authorities prohibited from sharing information with authorities conducting anticorruption investigations, and in five of 67 countries anticorruption authorities were prohibited from sharing information with administrative tax authorities. However, they could still share information with the authority responsible for investigating tax crimes (OECD and World Bank 2018).

Although it is now rare that countries explicitly prohibit information sharing between tax authorities and LEAs, with most introducing exceptions to any blanket prohibitions (indeed, there is no justification for blanket prohibitions), many jurisdictions would benefit from further progress in facilitating interagency information exchange.

Balancing Information Sharing and Privacy Considerations

Understandably, an overarching challenge has been the issue of confidentiality and, by extension, the broader concern about rights to privacy and data protection.[11] Tax authorities often abide by strict confidentiality rules to protect taxpayers' information.[12] Thus, in the process of lifting at least certain restrictions to ensure that LEAs access tax information and tax authorities access law enforcement information, the aim is to strike an appropriate balance between existing protections and information sharing to more effectively counteract crime while preserving legitimate individual rights to privacy.

Approaches to striking this balance fall on a spectrum. At one end of the spectrum, laws may grant certain authorities more generalized access to information, such as under a "direct access" model wherein authorized officials from designated agencies have special access to shared databases. At the other end of the spectrum, the law may be more prescriptive on how and under what conditions information may be exchanged.

Different legal frameworks may allow different approaches to information sharing. For example, laws may provide for direct access to records and databases, mandatory spontaneous sharing of information, voluntary spontaneous sharing of information, or sharing of information only upon request. These differences are reflected in practice. According to the 2017 OECD study on effective interagency cooperation, the ability of tax authorities to access information obtained by FIUs varied, with some countries permitting direct physical or electronic access, others providing for spontaneous sharing of relevant information by FIUs, and still others providing for no sharing at all (OECD 2017a).

Although it is tempting to simply broaden the circle of authorities with real-time access to information sources, any change should be pursued in a way that upholds confidentiality to preserve both the confidentiality of ongoing investigations and the privacy of the individuals involved. One way of achieving this goal is to require authorities handling confidential information to do so in a manner consistent with the requirements of the originating authority. For example, officials from the FIU, when accessing tax information, should be required to adhere to the same confidentiality rules as the tax authorities.[13] Moreover, there should be an assumption that any agency, as a "public body" representing the government, has "a duty to act consistently with" any convention on human rights to which the government adheres, including as it relates to privacy rights of individuals.[14]

Prescriptive Approaches to Information Sharing

Although some jurisdictions provide government agencies with broad access to information under certain circumstances,[15] others are more prescriptive, stipulating what, how, and under what conditions information can be exchanged.

Domestic laws may (1) restrict the types of information that can be shared (such as only information related to possible offenses of a certain level of severity); (2) stipulate that information sharing can take place only under certain conditions (such as upon request as opposed to spontaneously) and only when it will not seriously impair an investigation or when the requesting agency is able to show that the information is strictly necessary for the conduct of its mission or case; or (3) require specific procedures to be followed to obtain access to confidential information (such as only through a court order). See box 2.2 for country examples illustrating common parameters imposed on sharing of tax information.

Addressing Common Pitfalls in Legislating Information Sharing

Where a law incorporates restrictions and conditions on the sharing of information, as it often does, it is important that they do not render the law ultimately ineffectual. A 2018 report by the OECD and the World Bank surveying 67 countries underscored challenges arising from laws providing for cooperation (OECD and World Bank 2018). It lists five ways in which, despite having a legal basis for cooperation, laws could be insufficient or too restrictive:

1. Legislation can be too prescriptive, failing to adapt to new developments. For example, when it calls for information sharing to take place only in

BOX 2.2	Country Examples of Parameters around Information Sharing

New Zealand. The tax authorities follow a case-by-case approach to sharing information on serious crimes (Schlenther 2017). In doing so, they weigh whether the request is "fit for purpose," balancing privacy rights and the benefits for society of the information sharing. Relevant factors include the nature of the crime, the scope of the request, the intended use of the information, the ability of the tax authority to provide it, and the risk of error and misuse on the part of the recipient agency.

South Africa. Conditions and limitations on access to tax information from South Africa's tax authority, the South African Revenue Services (SARS), by the financial intelligence unit (FIU) and other law enforcement agencies are codified in law. Although the statutory language allows for a great deal of discretion by SARS, notably allowing spontaneous information sharing, it also provides specific parameters for it. In particular, under the Tax Administration Act,[a] the sharing of tax information must be necessary, relevant, and proportionate. It may be refused if SARS determines that the disclosure would seriously impair a tax investigation (although a court order could override it). The Financial Intelligence Centre Act[b] allows an FIU to have access to tax information from SARS as long as the information is required for the FIU to perform its duties and functions. All agency recipients of tax information from SARS are required to uphold the confidentiality of the information.

a. South Africa, Tax Administration Act, 2011, Act No. 28 of 2011, https://www.gov.za/sites/default/files/gcis
_document/201409/a282011.pdf.
b. South Africa, Financial Intelligence Centre Act, 2001, Act No. 38 of 2001, https://www.gov.za/sites/default/files/gcis
_document/201409/a38-010.pdf.

relation to a specific set of offenses, it runs the risk of preventing sharing about new offenses not previously accounted for.

2. Legislation can restrict the use of information shared between agencies. For example, it may allow the information shared to be used for investigative purposes, but not as admissible evidence in judicial proceedings (for more on this, see chapter 3). Such a restriction could hinder prosecution of the offenses being investigated.

3. Legislation can require burdensome preconditions for sharing information that add cost and time to investigations. For example, laws can require LEAs to launch a criminal proceeding or obtain a court order to access tax information pertinent to their investigation. Where these preconditions are deemed necessary and proportionate to safeguard confidentiality, the OECD and the World Bank recommend streamlining these processes by, for example, providing standardized templates to request a court order, as in the United States (OECD and World Bank 2018).[16]

4. Legislation can limit information sharing to that made "on request." This limitation creates a situation whereby an agency—such as a tax authority—becomes aware of information relevant to another agency's mandate, and yet it is not able to share the information because it has not been requested.[17]

This on-request approach requires a recipient agency to be aware of, and in some cases precisely specify, the relevant information held by another agency, ultimately reducing the chances that the relevant information reaches the recipient agency, or it may do so only after an unnecessary delay. To remediate this issue, legislators should consider limiting the use of on-request provisions and training tax authorities and LEAs on the types of specialized information possessed by other agencies that could be relevant to carrying out the functions of those LEAs and authorities.

5. Legislation can give officials the discretion to decide whether and when to share information, which can diminish the effectiveness of interagency cooperation. To ensure clarity and the appropriate use of discretion, the OECD and the World Bank recommend that agencies include clear internal policies on what types of information should be shared and when and how.

2.4.1.2 LAWS ON THE SCOPE AND DEFINITION OF TAX CRIMES

When the Financial Action Task Force (FATF) amended its recommendations in 2012 to include tax crimes as a predicate offense to money laundering,[18] it created an explicit legal link between the work of tax authorities—the authorities responsible for counteracting tax crimes—and the work of FIUs—the authorities responsible for counteracting money laundering.[19] However, in jurisdictions where tax crimes are defined too narrowly or imprecisely, the potential for cooperation and synergies between the relevant agencies can be low. Harmonization of the definition of tax crimes across countries has been slow, with criminalization at times varying greatly.[20] For example, some countries do not criminalize tax evasion.[21] Switzerland has a narrow definition (Lötscher and Buhr 2015) under which only certain types of tax fraud are criminalized, whereas tax "evasion" is considered a misdemeanor (Unger 2017).

Although the OECD has always maintained that having one universal definition for tax offenses does not support jurisdictional diversity, it does advocate that countries cover a range of offenses. The first principle listed in the OECD's *Fighting Tax Crime—The Ten Global Principles* is to "ensure Tax Offences are criminalized" (OECD 2017b), so the law is clear on which tax offenses are criminalized.[22] The OECD encourages jurisdictions to consider a range of behaviors, providing thresholds at which they should be criminalized: (1) "non-compliance offences (may apply irrespective of intent or result)," (2) "intentional tax offences," and (3) "specific offences."[23] To this, the report adds criminalizing accessory actions,[24] including by professional enablers, and the possibility of holding legal entities criminally liable for tax offenses (OECD 2017b). The expansion of the categories after the review of the laws establishing tax crimes may help bolster opportunities for interagency cooperation both domestically and internationally, and dual criminality under mutual legal assistance treaties (MLATs) should be considered in doing so.

Similarly, if countries adopt the same definition of "organized criminal group" as provided in the Palermo Convention[25] or provide similar coverage in their domestic laws, it would facilitate transnational investigations by enabling countries to issue and receive mutual legal assistance requests.

2.4.1.3 LAWS TO EXPAND TAX INFORMATION GATHERING

Even before information is exchanged, either between agencies domestically or internationally, an ability must be developed to gather the kind of intelligence that would alert authorities to possible criminal behavior.

On this front, a handful of tools for gathering and using tax information has emerged, especially in recent years, that may enhance the amount and scope of intelligence obtained by authorities. For example, in 2018 the OECD issued the *Model Mandatory Disclosure Rules for CRS Avoidance Arrangements and Opaque Offshore Structures* (OECD 2018a). These mandatory disclosure rules (MDRs) require intermediaries who are involved in promoting or structuring arrangements featuring certain "hallmarks" of tax avoidance to disclose information to the tax authorities. The purpose of these MDRs is "to provide tax administrations with information on arrangements that (purport to) circumvent the Common Reporting Standard . . . and on structures that disguise the beneficial owners of assets held offshore."[26] Moreover, countries around the world are implementing more broadly formulated MDRs, covering a variety of aggressive tax planning arrangements, following the OECD Base Erosion and Profit Shifting (BEPS) Action Plan (OECD 2015b).[27]

MDRs generally seek to capture *avoidance* strategies, not tax crimes. As a 2015 OECD report explains, MDRs are "intended to obtain early information about aggressive (or potentially abusive) tax planning which often takes advantage of loopholes in the law or uses legal provisions for purposes for which they were not intended." This differs from tax evasion and fraud, which "involves the direct violation of tax law and may feature the deliberate concealment of the true state of a taxpayer's affairs in order to reduce tax liability" (OECD 2015b, 85). Indeed, one issue raised is whether, to the extent MDRs may lead to a tax adviser or taxpayer disclosing a scheme that attracts legal consequences criminal in nature, they may run into due process concerns—in particular, the protection against self-incrimination (see OECD 2015b, 56–57, 85–86). Tax administrations must consider how to strike a balance so that MDRs do not force taxpayers or advisers to report information that incriminates them, but the OECD believes this balance can be struck.[28] Although MDRs do not target tax crimes per se, it may be that noncompliance with reporting obligations under MDRs can itself constitute a criminal offense. The OECD seems to suggest imposing dissuasive administrative penalties rather than necessarily creating a new criminal offense.[29] However, in some jurisdictions noncompliance may trigger criminal proceedings or constitute an offense.

The benefits of MDRs are, at least, threefold: (1) the early information may help detect unknown loopholes that policy makers can then address via legislative changes; (2) the obligation to report may also act as a deterrent, inducing advisers and taxpayers to hesitate before engaging in an "aggressive" arrangement; and (3) one indirect benefit is the general insight into commonly used structures (such as which legal entities are used, which types of assets, or which offshore jurisdictions). This bird's-eye view may help authorities better understand in general how to trace assets, follow the money, and unravel complex structures in future criminal investigations.

2.4.1.4 LAWS ON UNEXPLAINED WEALTH OR UNEXPLAINED REVENUE

"Unexplained wealth" is often understood to be wealth (property or assets, broadly defined) that a person holds or consumes that exceeds that person's (1) known income or (2) wealth (or both) and that was lawfully obtained or declared (see box 2.3 for examples of definitions of unexplained wealth). Ideally, the concept of "holding" wealth would be construed as broadly as possible to include holding property directly or indirectly via, for example, legal arrangements such as trusts. In other words, it should cover not only property that a person owns, but also property over which the person exercises effective control.

Although different terminology is used, such as "unexplained wealth,"[30] "unexplained assets,"[31] and "illicit enrichment,"[32] the concept can be used by both tax authorities and LEAs. Personal income tax, corporate income tax, property tax, value added tax (VAT) or sales tax, customs taxes, and other sources of tax information provide access to information on a person's income and wealth. The basic job of tax authorities is to research and detect unexplained wealth because any sign of undeclared or unduly minimized taxable revenue constitutes potential tax evasion. However, beyond tax violations, unexplained wealth or revenue in the context of tax verification may serve as an indicator of ill-gotten gains resulting from money laundering, corruption, or other financial crimes. It is essential that these red flags can be disclosed to LEAs. Moreover, FIUs

---

BOX 2.3	Definitions of Unexplained Wealth across Jurisdictions

Australia. Unexplained wealth arises when there are "reasonable grounds to suspect that the person's total wealth exceeds the value of the person's wealth that was lawfully acquired"—Proceeds of Crime Act 2002 (as amended), sec. 179B(1)(b).

Mauritius. Unexplained wealth includes "any property—(a) under the ownership of a person to an extent which is disproportionate to his emoluments and other income; (b) the ownership, possession, custody or control of which cannot be satisfactorily accounted for by the person who owns, possesses, has custody or control of the property; or (c) held by a person for another person to an extent which is disproportionate to the emoluments or other income of that other person and which cannot be satisfactorily accounted for"—The Good Governance and Integrity Reporting Act 2015, Act 31/2015, Government Gazette of Mauritius No. 122, December 10, 2015, sec. 2.

United Kingdom. One key condition for unexplained wealth is that "there are reasonable grounds for suspecting that the known sources of the respondent's lawfully obtained income would have been insufficient for the purposes of enabling the respondent to obtain the property"—UK, Criminal Finances Act 2017, sec. 362B(3).

receive suspicious transaction reports, offering insight into potentially unusual and large movements of money. This information can also be very useful to tax authorities because they could open their own tax verifications or investigations. Conversely, LEAs may, through audits, detect unexplained wealth in the context of corruption or money laundering investigations,[33] net worth analysis, or criminal proceedings for illicit enrichment offenses.

Therefore, laws authorizing or mandating authorities to detect and investigate "unexplained wealth" can be a useful tool to boost the exchange of information between tax authorities and LEAs (see box 2.4 for unexplained wealth order legislation adopted in the United Kingdom). Often, persons ostentatiously displaying their wealth, such as luxurious real estate or cars, attract the attention of the authorities. In addition, disgruntled spouses in divorce proceedings may also reveal previously hidden assets (see case 5 in appendix).

To assess whether wealth is truly *unexplained*, however, authorities would benefit from following a formal, methodical process. Broadly speaking, it requires at least two basic steps:

1. The authorities assess what is known (that is, what is "reasonably ascertainable from available information at the time"[34]) to be a person's lawfully obtained income and wealth arising from employment, assets, or otherwise. For public officials and politicians, some of this information should be readily available because they are paid directly by the

---

BOX 2.4   The United Kingdom's Unexplained Wealth Orders

In 2017, under the Criminal Finances Act, Section 362, the United Kingdom enacted legislation that shifts to the respondent the burden of proof of how certain suspicious assets were obtained. The "Unexplained Wealth Order" (UWO), which is in effect a new investigative power, is a court order issued to either an individual or a company suspected (on a "reasonable grounds" test) of involvement in serious criminality or having the status of a foreign (non-UK, non–European Economic Area) politically exposed person (PEP) or connected persons. Respondents must explain (within a time specified by the court) the origin of assets that appear to be disproportionate to their known income. When the High Court issues a UWO, it may also issue an interim freezing order for property if it considers it necessary to do so to avoid the risk that any recovery order subsequently obtained is frustrated. Failure of the respondent to comply with the requirements imposed by an UWO gives rise to a rebuttable presumption that the property is "recoverable" as the proceeds of a crime, and it means that LEAs can recover the property through existing civil recovery powers without requiring any further evidence of criminality.[a] If the respondent complies, the enforcement authority determines the next steps to be taken in relation to the property. UWOs go further than the United Kingdom's current civil recovery procedure by shifting the burden of proof to the accused, who must demonstrate that the asset was acquired legally.

a. Recently, a UWO was successfully applied to a UK businessman (NCA 2020).

government and, at least for the more senior officials, ideally have some obligation to declare assets upon assuming public roles. For private persons, this information may come from, for example, any known employers or tax returns, and is adjusted to account for any known nontaxable sources.

2. The authorities compare this lawfully obtained income and wealth with the property of the individual in question. "Property," first and foremost, refers to assets such as valuable immovable property (such as real estate), but also movable property (such as luxury cars, jewelry, clothes and accessories, and artwork). It should include both tangible and intangible property, such as interests in property through holdings, financial instruments, and so forth. Depending on the jurisdiction, this information may be available in land registries, company registries, vehicle registries, securities exchange commissions, and insurance records. The notion of property should also encompass other lifestyle indicators, such as spending and consumption or enjoyment of luxury goods such as yachts or planes, even though such property is less tangible because it is "consumed" but is nevertheless sometimes trackable. Spending on expensive dinners, exotic vacations, frequent gifts, or donations, where these can be traced to an individual, should also be considered. Gifts family members documented on paper are a common way to disguise the identity of the true beneficial owner of an asset.

The ability of tax authorities or LEAs to detect unexplained wealth may be supported by a variety of sources, and explicitly listing these can help authorities think resourcefully and strategically during this detection process. Persons may implicate themselves by boasting of their extravagant lifestyle on social media, thereby creating a publicly available record. Such a record has proven useful in the conviction of a high-level official and the accompanying forfeiture of his assets (Transparency International 2017). Social media, especially Instagram, also have played a role in the investigation, prosecution, and recovery of assets of other high-level officials (CNN 2020). Artificial intelligence algorithms may help authorities sift through the billions of social media posts to detect relevant information (for more on the role of data management and technology, see section 2.5).

Not only can officials implicate themselves—the public may also rally on social media to do the same. For example, a social media campaign was once launched under the hashtag #WeKnowYourSalary, prompting members of civil society to "audit top government officials by posting images of property and assets owned by these officials vis-a-vis their perceived salaries and allowances" (Obonyo 2018; see also Ching 2019). Facts, such as instances of the children of senior officials studying in exorbitantly expensive private schools and colleges, can sometimes be gleaned from social media.

Even if not on social media, certain signs of wealth are nonetheless readily visible, such as when a person's home address happens to be a conspicuously expensive piece of prime real estate, or when a person or the person's family is seen publicly with certain luxury goods such as cars, watches, and handbags (the accumulated costs of which can quickly reach into the thousands or even millions). Nonprofit organizations such as Transparency International and Global Witness have also compiled reports on such property, thereby drawing attention to such wealth, which can support investigations.[35] In addition, some countries require disclosure of high-value transactions such as payments for electricity, foreign travel, and the like (News18 2020).

Another visible activity is political campaigning. Where it is possible to estimate the amounts spent, questions may be raised about the sources of payment (especially when the payments appear to exceed funds disclosed under campaign finance laws). Whistleblower protections also can support individuals in reporting wrongdoing to law enforcement.[36]

In summary, authorities should be creative and resourceful in drawing on a variety of sources for the information needed to detect "unexplained wealth" and may even rely on interagency cooperation with securities exchange commissions and other asset registries to obtain additional information and trace the ownership of legal arrangements, properties, or legal persons, including registered corporations.

2.4.2 Exchange of Information on Beneficial Ownership

Under the Financial Action Task Force standards, a beneficial owner is the natural person who ultimately owns or controls a customer, legal person, or arrangement, or on whose behalf a transaction is carried out, and includes those who exercise ultimate effective control.

Beyond the ability to investigate a transaction, legal person, arrangement, or financial account, LEAs will need an effective, coherent framework to identify the ultimate natural person behind an opaque offshore scheme designed to hide his or her identity. Providing authorities with access to information identifying the beneficial owner is central to exposing hidden wealth. As stated by FATF, "the misuse of corporate vehicles could be significantly reduced if information regarding both the legal owner and the beneficial owner were readily available to authorities" (FATF 2014, 3). For this reason, the definition of a beneficial owner needs to be aligned across LEAs' functionalities and should enable identification of the natural person with ultimate ownership or effective control.

Widely adopted by national anti-money laundering (AML) frameworks, the FATF definition of beneficial ownership gives authorities the widest scope to determine the ultimate owner. Under the FATF standards, financial institutions and other designated businesses and professions falling under the scope of an AML framework have an obligation to identify the ultimate beneficial owner of the legal person, arrangement, or transaction with which they are involved. The identification and verification of beneficial ownership are thus an inherent feature of the customer due diligence process for a wide range of both financial and nonfinancial institutions and professional intermediaries, making them a good source of information for LEAs (Somare 2017).

Company registries are another source of beneficial ownership information available to LEAs, different types of asset registries (tangible and intangible), stock exchange commissions, and, of course, tax authorities. As noted by FATF, information collected by tax authorities on beneficial ownership and control of legal persons depends on the domestic tax regime and varies greatly across jurisdictions. Moreover, LEAs may not always be aware of the information collected and maintained by tax authorities (FATF 2019). Although the Global Forum's Exchange of Information on Request (EOIR) standard adopted the same definition of beneficial owner as FATF (IDB and OECD 2019), the differences in the adequacy and accuracy of the information collected by tax authorities remain a challenge.

Both standards identify options for implementing beneficial ownership requirements, including (1) establishing centralized registries made available to competent authorities or publicly accessible; (2) requiring companies to take reasonable measures to obtain and hold beneficial ownership information;[37] and (3) using existing beneficial ownership information sources, such as data collected by various authorities, financial institutions, or other designated businesses and professions. Centralized registers can play a useful role because they act as a single platform for the obligatory reporting of information. Depending on whether they are publicly accessible and on their searchability, these beneficial ownership registries may help confirm the connection between a natural person and a property, legal person, or arrangement, or they may reveal previously unknown connections.[38]

Although the alignment in definitions of beneficial ownership for AML and tax purposes recognizes the need for one standard across the board, there is still a need to address interagency cooperation in the implementation of a common beneficial ownership standard in practice. An evaluation of a country's legal framework is the appropriate starting point. See box 2.5 for some of the considerations in determining the effectiveness of a legal framework.

A whole-of-government approach to beneficial ownership is imperative. Typically, such cooperation would require an MoU. In addition, it can be carried out effectively only if the legal framework requires all agencies, financial institutions, and other designated businesses and professions to apply the same standard in collecting beneficial ownership information and this requirement is adequately enforced to ensure compliance.

In Kenya, both the Proceeds of Crime and Anti-Money Laundering Act (POCAMLA) and the Companies Act, 2015, adopt the FATF definition of a beneficial owner. However, lawyers have not been included as reporting persons for AML purposes, and they are not required to collect beneficial ownership information as part of customer due diligence (ESAAMLG 2017a). Because independent professionals are often involved in the establishment or administration of legal entities, they have vital insight into the real controllers of legal entities and arrangements. Thus, not imposing beneficial ownership obligations on them deprives country authorities of an essential source of information.

An effective legal framework must therefore cover all potential sources of beneficial ownership information and adequately enforce requirements to

BOX 2.5	Considerations in Implementing Beneficial Ownership Frameworks

When establishing a legal framework consistent with the Global Forum and Financial Action Task Force standards and ensuring it is effective in practice, a jurisdiction should consider doing the following:

- Conduct a gap analysis and review of the existing legal provisions.

- Determine what legal instrument should provide for beneficial ownership requirements and whether to cover all legal entities and arrangements.

- Identify who is obligated to collect information and report and maintain it.

- Introduce appropriate sanctions for noncompliance.

- To facilitate cooperation, create a framework that identifies and connects all competent authorities tasked with collecting beneficial ownership information.

- Ensure that competent authorities have appropriate access to beneficial ownership information and ensure it is accurate, complete, and up to date.

collect it to give LEAs the best chance of identifying and prosecuting the real owner of an asset or transaction. The collection and sharing of adequate, accurate, up-to-date beneficial ownership information depend on countries ensuring that they have enabling legal frameworks, possess enhanced capacity (in both staffing and infrastructure) to manage and verify data such as through centralized registers, and are able to enforce requirements for financial institutions and other designated businesses and professions.

Finally, legislative impediments to interagency cooperation in the collection and sharing of beneficial ownership information should be addressed and include (1) any potential differences in the definition of beneficial owner in legislation providing for all forms of asset registers, including securities, vehicles, land and property, companies, tax information collection, and anti-money laundering/countering the financing of terrorism (AML/CFT) reporting by financial institutions and other designated businesses and professions; (2) the determinants of effective control—these should be broad and could include any significant creditors or family members of the beneficial owner; and (3) the legal obligation of LEAs, financial institutions, or other designated businesses or professions to share beneficial ownership information that is accurate and timely.

2.5 Operational Aspects of Cooperation at the Domestic Level

Multiagency coordination is required at both the policy level and the operational level. At the policy level, it will ensure the goals and objectives of agencies are met. At the operational level, it will enable sharing of expertise to build capacity to ensure that information is shared smoothly and in the desired format and to provide for adequate resources dedicated to facilitating cooperation (notably by assigning operational-level officers to the task). Officers at the relevant agencies should receive clear guidance on how information will be exchanged and used and who their key contacts in each agency will be.

2.5.1 Formal and Informal Models for Cooperation

Agencies tackling financial crimes are often interdependent, with their mandates and objectives at times intersecting or even overlapping (Schlenther 2017). As a result, coordination is needed to set a clear agenda and delineate the primary roles of the agencies involved. Of the several approaches to cooperation between tax authorities and LEAs, all should promote greater understanding of each agency's mandate and the type of information it collects. Ultimately, no matter the approach, effective cooperation should facilitate access to pertinent information by the relevant agencies and lead to the identification and investigation of potentially criminal conduct.

2.5.1.1 MODELS FOR FORMAL COOPERATION

Formal tools for cooperation—typically involving entering into some type of agreement or coordination of processes—include MoUs, service-level agreements (SLAs), coordination arrangements,[39] joint investigative teams, joint training interventions, and joint committees to coordinate policies in areas of shared responsibilities.

Memoranda of Understanding

An MoU both comprehensively lays out the structure of collaboration between agencies and facilitates an effective exchange of information (GTPC 2018). In doing so, it identifies the basic elements of the cooperative process that will guide officials in their day-to-day tasks. That content should be detailed and compliant with applicable legal provisions. However, MoUs should not formulate a binding legal obligation for any of the agencies involved (GTPC 2018). Instead, and more important, MoUs should lay out the legal limitations on the exchange of information between agencies.

Several countries have used MoUs to formalize interagency cooperation. For example, in 2016 the Zambia Revenue Authority (ZRA) and the Zambian Financial Intelligence Centre signed an MoU to facilitate the exchange of information between the two agencies (ESAAMLG 2017b). This agreement has resulted in increased access to tax information held by the ZRA and the recovery of $2.4 million in 2018 (ESAAMLG 2017b).

Service-Level Agreements

Agencies may also consider SLAs, which are agreements between agencies to exchange services. They may recognize and take advantage of a specific skill or area of expertise offered by an agency while preventing duplication of efforts. For example, in the context of the Proceeds of Crime Act 2002 in the United Kingdom, SLAs may cover the cooperation and exchange of services between agencies in an investigation, in preserving assets, in obtaining and enforcing confiscation orders, and in confiscation matters. They are intended to serve as a general guide to cooperation between the parties and to allow the necessary flexibility in any activities undertaken between them. SLAs set out the shared aims of the parties to implement the Proceeds of Crime Act 2002 and to clarify the realistic expectations and intentions of the parties to it.[40]

Joint Investigative Teams and Joint Task Forces

For large, complex financial investigations into corruption, money laundering, or tax crimes, joint investigative teams (JITs)[41] are highly effective in ensuring that the investigation, prosecution, and recovery of proceeds are handled efficiently and thoroughly (GTPC 2018). These teams or task forces can be employed by agencies both domestically and across borders. A JIT as a tool for cooperation enables direct and immediate sharing of information, often providing even wider access than available in other circumstances (GTPC 2018).

In addition to sharing information, JITs enable investigations to draw on a wider range of skills and experience from investigators with different backgrounds and training. They also may avoid duplication arising from parallel investigations and increase efficiency by allocating responsibility for different aspects of an investigation to competent officials from each agency on the basis of their experience and legal powers. Finally, JITs turn what is usually a fragmented investigative process into a connected one, creating a clear, comprehensive picture of the conduct at issue. Many countries make use of these strategies.[42]

JITs of competent authorities (including judicial, law enforcement, and certain tax authorities) can be established for a limited duration and purpose such as carrying out criminal investigations of a specific target or a specific series of crimes,[43] or they can be longer-standing and broader in scope. See box 2.6 for country examples of long-standing JITs, as well as case 10 in the appendix.

In setting up JITs, the relevant agencies will need to consult with the prosecution authorities and judges to determine the applicable rules for procedures and evidence. The objective is to minimize the likelihood of any delays in prosecution, particularly when formal requests for information may be needed because information initially exchanged by JIT participants is not admissible in court for procedural reasons.

The OECD has identified instances in which the use of evidence obtained through tax authorities cannot be accepted in a criminal case because "deploying civil powers for the purposes of the criminal investigation may constitute an abuse of power and any evidence obtained may be inadmissible in court" (OECD 2017b, 31). As a result, "procedural safeguards are of particular importance . . . where the tax administration conducts civil examinations or audits and also has the authority to conduct criminal investigations" (OECD 2017b, 31). Thus, in some

---

BOX 2.6   Country Examples of Long-Standing Joint Investigative Teams

Kenya. The Multi-Agency Team (MAT) is a standing joint investigative team (JIT) in Kenya. It is composed of eight authorities—including law enforcement agencies (LEAs), the tax authority, and the office of the president—with an established mandate and the rubber stamp of a presidential directive (Nyaga, n.d.). By 2016, MAT had jointly led 13 cases and investigations, and approximately $300 million has been recovered or preserved as a result (Nyaga, n.d.).

Australia. Another long-standing JIT, Project Wickenby was established under the auspices of the Australian Tax Office (ATO) in 2005 (Schlenther 2017). The longest-running joint agency investigation initiated by the Australian government to combat offshore tax evasion, it was run by the ATO, the Australian Securities and Investment Commission, the Australian Federal Police, and the Australian Crime Commission. As a result of this joint effort, 2,800 audits were carried out, 18 people were imprisoned, and $A 553 million was recovered (Chenoweth, Buffini, and Low 2011).

Mauritius. The Anti-Money Laundering/Countering the Financing of Terrorism Coordination Taskforce consists of representatives of seven agencies, including counterterrorism, police, the tax authority, anticorruption, the Integrity Reporting Services Agency (for confiscation of unexplained wealth), and the prosecuting authority to exchange information and coordinate the investigation of complex predicate offense schemes and their concomitant money laundering, terrorism financing, and tax crimes. Prosecutorial advice on the evidential standards required to secure convictions is given at each stage of an investigation. Although statutory limitations affect the revenue authority's ability to share information, MoUs between relevant LEAs are able to compensate in cases where money laundering is suspected.

---

cases, further independent evidence will be required. For example, under South Africa's Tax Administration Act, if there are indications during a tax audit that tax offenses may have been committed, the case must be referred to the South African Revenue Services (SARS) criminal investigation team.[44] Thereafter, the audit and criminal investigation proceed separately.

Moreover, teams must ensure that each agency is compliant with its legal mandate, manages the process of obtaining and handling evidence as required, and respects the rights of a suspect. This is particularly important because any errors may result in challenges and possible failures during prosecution. In 17 countries reviewed by the OECD and the World Bank, although judges and prosecutors are not involved in the investigation process, they are tasked with reviewing the documentation to determine whether to proceed with the case (OECD and World Bank 2018). Where this is the case, interagency cooperative teams are advised to involve the prosecution authority in the early stages of an investigation to ensure that due process is followed and sufficient evidence is obtained to increase the chances of successful prosecution (OECD and World Bank 2018).

Similarly, joint task forces often are set up for certain specific purposes, which may limit the purposes for which information can be further disseminated. For example, FIUs may only be able to use or disseminate tax information received in the context of a joint task force for the specific purposes of that task force, limiting its use and dissemination beyond it. Moreover, once the task force no longer exists, FIUs will no longer have access to that tax information and will not be able to capture the financial footprint it was able to create using that information.

Joint Training Interventions

Cross-functional training interventions make officials aware of the related functions, skills, knowledge, and types of information collected by other agencies. Joint training programs, involving officials from more than one agency or led by experts from different agencies, are an important opportunity for officials to build personal relationships across agencies and benefit from each other's experience and expertise in dealing with common problems. These programs are also a useful platform for sharing information on trends in financial crime, guidance on investigative techniques, and best practices in managing cases (GTPC 2018). Ultimately, joint training programs ensure that personnel working in one agency can recognize indicators of crimes outside of their specific mandates and that they then can refer those to the competent agency.

To raise the awareness of their participants, joint training sessions should extensively cover the legal frameworks for exchange of information between different agencies because the frameworks may vary significantly and give rise to some limitations in practice. Once they are acquainted with the basics of criminal law and procedure, tax officials will understand what information may be useful to LEAs in initiating an investigation of corruption, money laundering, or tax fraud. Similarly, by teaching LEAs the techniques of tax law and investigations, such programs can ensure that the relevant information arising from a criminal investigation is shared with tax authorities.

Joint Committees to Coordinate Policies in Areas of Shared Responsibilities

Over and above investigative task forces, which have a more operational mandate, countries may also establish more permanent policy coordinating bodies or committees. These joint committees might include a variety of public and private stakeholders with the objective of ensuring that the activities of agencies complement each other and that permanent platforms for cooperation are established. At the same time, this enhanced cooperation can establish and strengthen trust, which is central to promoting information sharing. In Kenya, for example, the AML/CFT Round Table Meeting gives authorities an opportunity to train reporting entities and other authorities while enabling information sharing (GTPC 2018). Together with key authorities such as the Office of the Attorney General and Department of Justice, the Ethics and Anti-Corruption Commission, the Kenya Revenue Authority, and the Director of Public Prosecutions, the forum includes the Asset Recovery Agency, the Insurance Regulatory Authority, banks, and mobile money service providers (GTPC 2018).

Public-Private Partnerships

As financial crime techniques become even more complex, public-private partnerships can enable an exchange of information on these techniques and bridge the gap between law enforcement and private sector entities. In Australia, the Fintel Alliance[45] brings together 29 members of the public sector and private sector (domestic and international) with the twin objectives of increasing the resilience of the financial sector to exploitation by criminals and supporting law enforcement investigations into serious crime, including tax crimes.

The alliance helped the Australian Federal Police gain a better understanding of financial products and services, and financial industry partners used the outcomes of cases to mitigate the risks associated with fraud, including tax fraud. The operations hub of the alliance allows information exchange and real-time analysis of information, and an innovation hub gives partners an opportunity to co-design and test new technology for gathering and analyzing financial intelligence.[46]

A similar initiative in the European Union is the Europol Financial Intelligence Public Private Partnership Steering Group (EFIPPP), comprising experts from banks, FIUs, and competent authorities from EU and non-EU countries (Riondet 2018). FIUs are also exploring the use of artificial intelligence and data analytics tools to improve transaction monitoring. Meanwhile, some jurisdictions are initiating or increasing the use of artificial intelligence software to process criminal databases (criminal records), financial databases (suspicious transactions from the FIU), tax declarations, and social networks, including to detect unexplained wealth.[47]

2.5.1.2 MODELS FOR INFORMAL COOPERATION

Opportunities to cooperate through informal networks can facilitate the establishment of working relationships, giving authorities an opportunity to communicate on an ongoing basis. These communications can be particularly useful for urgent matters or where one LEA requires guidance in the selection of the appropriate formal cooperative route. Some channels for informal cooperation are described in the following sections (GTPC 2018).

Secondments

Seconding staff from a LEA to the tax authority, or vice versa, can provide the receiving unit with expertise and skills and the secondee with a learning opportunity. Secondments can also establish informal relationships between key staff in the agencies involved.

Use of Shared Databases

Although access to information is discussed extensively later in this chapter, in general the use of shared databases requires some communication between authorities to coordinate the management and security of those databases. That communication may improve understanding of the type of information relevant to each authority and encourage authorities to share information for the sake of efficiency. Over the years, LEAs and tax authorities have created shared databases and collaborated—about leaked data or whistleblower information—in some cases provided by international alliances and civil society organizations (CSOs).

Since 2013, the International Consortium of Investigative Journalists (ICIJ) has published information leaked from over 785,000 entities through the Paradise Papers, Bahamas Leaks, Luxembourg Leaks, Panama Papers, and Mauritius Leaks, among others (see box 2.7 for examples of ICIJ investigations and publications used by criminal and tax investigators). In many countries,

---

BOX 2.7	International Consortium of Investigative Journalists: Following the Leaks

Luxembourg Leaks. A financial scandal revealed in November 2014, Lux Leaks was based on confidential information about tax rulings in Luxembourg overseen by PricewaterhouseCoopers from 2002 to 2010 to benefit its clients. The investigation eventually made public tax rulings for over 300 multinational companies based in Luxembourg. The Lux Leaks disclosures attracted international attention and debate about tax avoidance schemes in Luxembourg and elsewhere. This scandal contributed to the implementation of measures aimed at reducing tax dumping and regulating tax avoidance schemes benefiting multinational companies.

Panama Papers. The Panama Papers, published in April 2016, were an unprecedented leak of 11.5 million files from the database of the world's fourth-largest offshore law firm, Mossack Fonseca. The records were obtained from an anonymous source by the German newspaper *Süddeutsche Zeitung*, which shared them with the International Consortium of Investigative Journalists (ICIJ). The ICIJ then shared them with a large network of international partners, including the *Guardian* and the BBC. The documents contain previously private personal financial information about wealthy individuals and public officials. Although offshore business entities are legal, reporters found that some of the Mossack Fonseca shell corporations were used for criminal purposes, including fraud, tax evasion, and evading international sanctions.

Malta Leaks. In May 2017, a data leak revealed information about 70,000 offshore companies in Malta. Reportedly, multiple German companies and up to 2,000 German taxpayers were registered in Malta, and the data revealed how corporations and private persons on the Mediterranean island used these companies to bypass taxes in Germany.

Paradise Papers. In the fall of 2017, a data leak revealed over 13 million documents about the offshore financial affairs of hundreds of politicians, multinationals, celebrities, and high-net-worth individuals. Significant information shed light on the sophisticated mechanisms used by legal firms, financial institutions, and accountants specializing in jurisdictions that adopt offshore tax rules to attract money.

(continued next page)

BOX 2.7	International Consortium of Investigative Journalists: Following the Leaks *(continued)*

Luanda Leaks. A data leak of more than 715,000 financial and business records exposed the financial dealings of Isabel dos Santos, daughter of former Angolan president José Eduardo dos Santos. The leaks, published in January 2020, documented emails, internal memos, contracts, consultant reports, tax returns, private audits, and videos of business meetings from dos Santos's companies. They found that dos Santos, her husband, and their intermediaries built a business empire of more than 400 companies and subsidiaries in 41 countries. Over a period of 10 years, these companies secured consultancies, loans, public works contracts, and licenses from the Angolan government.

Pandora Papers. The most recent of the ICIJ investigations, the Pandora Papers, published in October 2021, are the result of 11.9 million records leaked from 14 offshore service providers. The records implicated more than 330 politicians from over 90 countries and territories, as well as 130 billionaires and countless celebrities and other high-profile individuals. The data and the subsequent investigation by the ICIJ and 150 media outlets around the world revealed unprecedented information about the beneficial ownership of entities and arrangements registered in secrecy jurisdictions, including in Belize; the British Virgin Islands; Hong Kong SAR, China; Panama; and the United States (South Dakota). Within hours of publication of the Pandora Papers, several countries—including Australia, Brazil, the Czech Republic, Mexico, Pakistan, Panama, Spain, and Sri Lanka—indicated that they would be opening investigations of the information made available through the leaks.

Source: International Consortium of Investigative Journalists, https://www.icij.org/investigations/.

prosecutors or LEAs have often opened criminal investigations on the basis of media releases in which the facts reported led to suspicion or evidence that a crime was committed. In turn, these authorities may share information with tax authorities. Conversely, tax authorities launch tax audits based on CSO reports and share findings that could lead LEAs to open criminal investigations.

Jurisdictional opinions about the use of these data to prosecute suspects vary greatly. In Germany, this practice is acceptable, and, in fact, authorities pay for such information (DW 2017). Similarly, in the United States, the Department of Justice charged four defendants with wire fraud, tax fraud, money laundering, and other offenses in connection with their role in pushing forward schemes uncovered by the Panama Papers (US Department of Justice 2018). Switzerland, however, rejected invitations from Germany to analyze the leaked data from the Panama Papers, and the Swiss Office of the Attorney General cited its restrictive regulations on how it could receive and use evidence (SwissInfo 2019).

In 2016, the Australian Criminal Intelligence Commission and Australian Taxation Office worked closely with the Serious Financial Crime Taskforce to analyze the data arising from the Panama Papers and secure additional intelligence to support their investigations (ACIC 2016). In 2019, the Australian High Court unanimously ruled that legal privilege could not be claimed over data leaked through the Paradise Papers, enabling the ATO to use the emails, board briefing notes, and legal advice related to a 2014 corporate restructuring to determine whether any taxes had been evaded (Smyth 2019).

The "Lagarde list" of individuals with hidden accounts in HSBC Switzerland revealed the limitations of using leaked data (Palin 2016). Following the Panama Papers leak, in the United Kingdom, Her Majesty's Revenue and Customs (HMRC) agency cross-checked the data through its analytical digital tool, Connect, which contains over 22 billion lines of data, including customers' self-assessment returns and property and financial data (HMRC 2019). Although over 9,000 residents of the United Kingdom were on the list, HMRC was able to charge only one individual with tax evasion due to concerns that the data could not meet the standard of evidence deemed admissible in court (HMRC 2019).

The usefulness of any data derived from whistleblowers or information leaks will always depend on whether the data constitute sufficient evidence to warrant a criminal conviction and whether they can be matched with data in domestic files that have been legally obtained. In most cases, the data will act as a red flag for authorities to investigate further. This may entail securing more intelligence or interviewing suspects and their professional advisers.

Interagency Centers of Intelligence and Fusion Centers

Interagency centers in the form of fusion centers and centers of intelligence entail the inclusion of one representative or more from each unit engaged in investigative efforts and information sharing. This integrated approach combines interagency resources and enables sharing of information within the boundaries of the law. These centers will have a clear mandate and division of roles, but they need not be established through any legal framework. In Australia, the National Criminal Intelligence Fusion Centre was launched in 2010 to bring together information, skills, knowledge, data, and technology across government departments (Schlenther 2017). The fusion center approach integrated information and intelligence on high-risk areas (Schlenther 2017).

2.5.2 Establishing a Fluid, Secure System for Exchanging Information

A legal framework that provides the policy tools for and legitimizes effective interagency cooperation should be supplemented by procedures to operationalize in practice such exchanges within and between agencies. To achieve this objective, authorities should conduct a stock-taking exercise, taking into account legislative, administrative, and tactical considerations to determine the operational parameters for exchanging information. Beyond mapping out the responsibilities of each agency and method of information sharing, countries should assess the security of information-sharing platforms, their confidentiality, and their compliance with data protection requirements. Where "a fluid system of sharing financial information and intelligence is established, a country will make more effective use of financial data, thus becoming more effective in combating money laundering," corruption, and tax crimes (FATF 2012b, 7).

In establishing robust data hosting platforms, LEAs must respect the legal protections to which suspects are entitled in access to their information. To ensure that legal protections are upheld, information received in the course of interagency cooperation must not be accessible by unauthorized persons, and information security management must be guaranteed (OECD 2015a). For example, the common transmission system (CTS)[48] enables the automatic exchange of information between hundreds of jurisdictions and thousands of financial institutions.[49] Resources, such as the file preparation and encryption user guides, are prepared to enable smooth and secure information sharing (OECD 2018b). See box 2.8 on the CTS standard.

Data and information management is critical because the lack of secure, reliable systems may compromise cooperation within and across jurisdictions by reducing trust. Procedural safeguards, including those designed to prevent any undue access or sharing, go a long way toward fostering trust in a system (OECD 2015a). The OECD has developed a model protocol that can be used and adapted in tax matters by interested jurisdictions (OECD 2015c).

BOX 2.8   The Common Transmission System Standard

The Common Transmission System (CTS) was launched in 2017 and currently supports the automatic exchange of common reporting standard (CRS) information, country-by-country reports, and tax rulings by more than 100 jurisdictions.

The CRS calls on jurisdictions to obtain information from their financial institutions and automatically exchange that information with other jurisdictions on an annual basis. It sets out the financial account information to be exchanged, the financial institutions required to report, the different types of accounts and taxpayers covered, as well as common due diligence procedures to be followed by financial institutions. The CRS has four parts:

- A model Competent Authority Agreement (CAA) providing the international legal framework for the exchange of CRS information

- A common reporting standard

- Commentaries on the CAA and the CRS

- The CRS XML Schema

In February 2020, the Organisation for Economic Co-operation and Development (OECD) released information technology formats and guidance to support technical implementation of the OECD's CTS for the exchange of information by tax administrations. The CTS also supports a wide range of other exchanges, including on-request and spontaneous exchanges, as well as the transmission of information pertaining to mutual agreement procedures, the OECD's Treaty Relief and Compliance Enhancement (TRACE) initiative, and other forms of cooperation.

Data can be made available using a cloud server, with secure storage and subject to data privacy and confidentiality requirements (OECD 2015c). Because authorities must ensure they are using similar systems and interfaces to store data, shared systems could "be designed and developed with interoperability in mind" (OECD 2015c). The accuracy, adequacy, and reliability of the information fed into a shared database must also be verified. Databases may include more comprehensive and exhaustive data at the investigative stage because tax authorities, FIUs, and LEAs are looking for leads to develop an investigation and can often share information with their counterparts through application of existing legislation or protocols. The management of information at the prosecution/judicial stage has to be directed more toward the possible charges under consideration and take into account the legal limitations provided in criminal legislation and procedures.

But simply collecting data is not enough. Countries may wish to consider using new technologies in upgrading data pooling and analysis systems that could provide ease of administration, including, potentially, blockchain, artificial intelligence, and data mining.

Agencies need tools that will allow them to identify and track the links between the information collected. Such tools will require additional capacities for connecting and analyzing databases such as data analytics. Policy makers should support interoperability by requiring agencies to link their databases and triangulate the data collected. Smart technology such as artificial intelligence and neural networks could help in triangulating the data in, for example, company registries, tax databases, land registries, and other financial records. Some tax authorities and LEAs now use data mining, artificial intelligence, and deep learning to cross-analyze data they already have with data from external sources, including that derived from the automatic exchange of tax information and social media (TFI Info 2020).

The OECD's recently published *Tax Crime Investigation Maturity Model* (OECD 2020), a self-assessment diagnostic tool, is intended to help jurisdictions understand where they stand in the implementation of the OECD's *Fighting Tax Crime—The Ten Global Principles* (OECD 2017b), based on a set of empirically observed indicators. By setting out indicators for each increasing level of maturity, the model also charts an evolutionary path for future progress toward the most cutting-edge practices in tax crime investigation across four levels of maturity: Emerging, Progressing, Established, and Aspirational. Assessing the current level of interagency coordination domestically and internationally across the value chain of the law enforcement process, from initial intelligence gathering for detection and prevention to investigating, prosecuting, and eventually recovering the criminal proceeds, is an integral part of the self-assessment.

The effectiveness of interagency coordination for countering illicit financial flows is specifically examined during the self-assessment process. The model looks at interagency coordination across multiple dimensions, including a joint national risk assessment, a joint risk mitigation plan with shared responsibility, an improved legal and operational framework for reporting and information sharing, use of enhanced cooperation by way of an MoU, a joint investigation, multiagency training, an interagency center of intelligence, and a joint operations and multiagency taskforce. Based on the self-assessment, a jurisdiction can adopt reform initiatives to improve interagency coordination to fight financial crimes more effectively.

Notes

1. For definitions, see United Nations Convention against Corruption, art. 15, and Organisation for Economic Co-operation and Development (OECD) Convention on Combating Bribery of Foreign Public Officials in International Business Transactions, art. 1. The reasons for and ways in which to engage in bribery vary. Although these can include payments to secure an official act (such as a payment to an official to certify a document, clear a consignment, or jump the queue), bribes are not limited to a financial inducement. For example, authorities may agree to provide some sort of benefit in return for a specific act, service, or consideration, or for refraining to act.
2. In some countries, the payment of "commissions" to foreign officials was lawful, recorded, and tax-deductible until ratification of the OECD Convention on Combating Bribery of Foreign Public Officials in International Business Transactions.
3. Some commonly used methods to mask inappropriate payments are to record them as salaries, consultancy fees, payments for goods and services that ultimately are not delivered or rendered, and marketing expenses.
4. See Schlenther (2017, 94), who states: "The ATO's [Australian Tax Office's] role is explained by 'the profit driven nature of organised crime' and the fact that the necessary skills are available to the ATO to help with the identification of unexplained wealth that is generated through the proceeds of crime." Also see OECD (2017b, 58), which states: "Furthermore, the various agencies may each have unique information or investigative and enforcement powers that can enhance another agency's investigation of a particular crime. This makes co-operation amongst the relevant agencies particularly important and beneficial." See the discussion of unexplained wealth orders later in this chapter.
5. See FATF recommendations 20 and 23.
6. As described by the National Crime Agency (UK), "Financial Intelligence, The Impact of SARs in Reducing Crime," https://www.ukciu.gov.uk/(Objnmzrzvyjwpwrqvvfzdg2u)/Information/Info.aspx.
7. See EU Directive 2016/680 of the European Parliament and of the Council, April 27, 2016, on (1) the protection of natural persons with regard to the processing of personal data by competent authorities for the purposes of the prevention, investigation, detection, or prosecution of criminal offenses or the execution of criminal penalties and (2) the free movement of such data. The directive repeals Council Framework Decision 2008/977/JHA.
8. For example, the Australian Taxation Office (ATO) refers suspected criminal cases, including suspected corruption offenses as described by United Nations Convention against Corruption (UNCAC), art. 15-25, to the Australian Federal Police (AFP) for investigation and prosecution as appropriate. In cases in which foreign bribery is suspected during a taxation audit or investigation, the deductions claimed for those expenses are disallowed under the Income Tax Assessment Act 1997, sec. 26-52, and the case is referred to the AFP for investigation and prosecution as a criminal offense under Division 70 of the Criminal Code Act 1995.

9. As discussed in this chapter, the appropriate legal framework must also be in place to enable exchanges with counterparts in other jurisdictions. It is important to consider in some jurisdictions whether the scope of the definition of tax crimes should be clarified or extended. Narrow definitions will often reduce the potential scope of the international exchange of information, with jurisdictions strictly applying the principle of reciprocity.

10. See United Kingdom: Criminal Finances Act 2017, sec. 362A*ff*, http://www.legislation.gov .uk/ukpga/2017/22/contents (which represents a rather novel approach to laws that target "unexplained wealth" or "illicit enrichment"); Australia: Proceeds of Crime Act 2002, as amended, sec. 179A*ff*; Mauritius: The Good Governance and Integrity Reporting Act 2015, Act 31/2015, Government Gazette of Mauritius No. 122, December 10, 2015; Zimbabwe: Parliament, Money Laundering and Proceeds of Crime Amendment Bill, H.B. 4, 2019, https:// www.law.co.zw/download/money-laundering-and-proceeds-of-crime-amendment-bill-2019/; Trinidad and Tobago: The Civil Asset Recovery and Management and Unexplained Wealth Bill, 2019, Bill Essentials No. 12, 2018–19, April 2, 2019, http://www.ttparliament.org/documents /2810.pdf.

11. This issue is especially relevant to information exchange at the international level, which is discussed in chapter 4. As the automatic exchange of information grew more widespread, calls for protection of "taxpayers' rights" grew louder to ensure that a balance is struck. See US Internal Revenue Service, "Taxpayer Bill of Rights," https://www.irs.gov/taxpayer-bill-of -rights (adopted in 2014).

12. See, for example, OECD (2012, 5), which states: "Confidentiality of taxpayer information has always been a fundamental cornerstone of tax systems."

13. For example, South Africa requires both its tax authority, the South African Revenue Services, as well as other persons authorized to handle tax information, including the FIU, to abide by the same requirements under South Africa's 2011 Tax Administration Act. See South Africa, Tax Administration Act, 2011, Act No. 28 of 2011, sec. 67(2), https://www.gov.za/sites /default/files/gcis_document/201409/a282011.pdf.

14. See UK, Hajiyeva v. National Crime Agency, [2020] EWCA Civ 108 (February 5, 2020), at para. 52. In the context of a case about an "unexplained wealth order": "Further, the judge bore in mind that any information which was provided by the appellant would be provided to the NCA which, as a public body, had a duty to act consistently with the European Convention on Human Rights, and was bound to comply with the Overseas Security and Justice Assistance guidance which included specific processes for deciding whether disclosure to a third party would give rise to an impermissible risk. There was no suggestion that the NCA would use or disclose information sought otherwise than for the purposes of the statute . . . ; and no further safeguards, whether by way of undertakings from the NCA or otherwise . . . , were required."

15. Bulk data sharing has been considered and, under specified circumstances, adopted by the Australian FIU, the Australian Transaction Reports and Analysis Center (AUSTRAC). Where large fraud cases arise and involve several individuals, it may not be efficient to share information on a case-by-case basis. Most recently, Australian authorities were able to detect fraudulent attempts to use fake identities to access the funds distributed to citizens as part of COVID-19 stimulus measures. Using advanced analytics, authorities assessed the common characteristics associated with that fraud to identify when it may arise, and this information was shared with LEAs to uncover fraud. After filtering data through the identified

characteristics, the authorities were able to use the bulk sharing of information to detect fraud on an ongoing basis.

16. See US Department of Justice, "2012 Criminal Tax Manual," sec. 42, https://www.justice.gov /sites/default/files/tax/legacy/2015/03/26/CTM%20TOC.pdf.

17. Both on-request and spontaneous information sharing are relatively common. For example, according to Ghana's anti-money laundering legislation, the tax authority must spontaneously share all relevant information about suspicious transactions with the FIU. By contrast, in Finland the FIU can receive information from other agencies, including the tax authority, only upon request. See, for example, Schlenther (2017).

18. See OECD (2018a), which highlights this moment as an important change for relations between FIUs and tax administrations.

19. Money laundering, which is itself a criminal offense, occurs when people aim to dissimulate the illicit origin of their funds. Money laundering is thus "predicated" on the commission of a distinct prior offense that gave rise to the funds now being "laundered."

20. For example, in surveys conducted of European Union Member States, widely differing approaches and terminology were found. See Unger (2017) and Unger et al. (2018).

21. See OECD (2017b, 15), which finds that in some jurisdictions, acts of tax evasion may be criminalized only in narrow circumstances if there are particular "aggravating circumstances such as if the amount of tax evaded exceeds a certain threshold, if the offense is committed repeatedly, when taxable income is actively concealed, or when records or evidence are deliberately falsified."

22. The second edition of *Fighting Tax Crime—The Ten Global Principles* was published in 2021: https://www.oecd.org/tax/crime/fighting-tax-crime-the-ten-global-principles-second-edition -006a6512-en.htm.

23. OECD (2017b, 15). Examples of (1), noncompliance offenses, are "Failure to provide required information, document or return," "Failure to register for tax purposes," "Failure to keep records," "Keeping incorrect records," "Making a false statement," and "Non-payment of a tax liability." Examples of (2), intentional tax offenses, are "Destroying records," "Deliberate failure to comply with tax law to obtain financial advantage," "Evading tax or receiving refunds by fraud or illegal practices," "Intentional reduction of tax using false documents, fictitious invoices," "Counterfeit or forged documents to reduce tax," "Intentionally or by gross negligence providing misleading information in a tax return to obtain tax advantage," "Fraudulently obtaining refund / credit," "Tax evasion in aggravated circumstances such as considerable financial benefit or conducted in a methodical manner," "Theft from or defrauding the government," "Obstructing an official of the tax authority," and "Accessory offences." Examples of (3), specific offences, are "Entering an arrangement that would make person unable to pay tax," "Committing tax evasion as member of a gang," "Commercial commission of tax evasion," "Illegal use of zappers or sale suppression softwar," and "Identity theft."

24. Which is, according to OECD (2017b, 15), "the act of aiding, abetting, facilitating or enabling the commission of a tax offence by others, or conspiracy to commit a tax offence."

25. United Nations Convention against Transnational Organized Crime and the Protocols Thereto (2000).

26. Organisation for Economic Co-operation and Development, "Mandatory Disclosure Rules for Addressing CRS Avoidance Arrangements and Opaque Offshore Structures, Questions and Answers," https://www.oecd.org/tax/exchange-of-tax-information/mandatory-disclosure -rules-questions-and-answers.pdf.

27. See, for example, EU Council Directive 2018/822/EU, May 25, 2018.
28. Also see Mexico's approach (ITR 2020); the comment of the Chartered Institute on Taxation (CIOT) on the OECD's MDR rules (Curran 2018); and Bloomberg on the European Union's MDR rules (Bloomberg Tax 2019).
29. See, for example, the section on "Consequences of compliance and non-compliance" in OECD (2015b, 56).
30. In, for example, Australia, Mauritius, Trinidad and Tobago, the United Kingdom, and Zimbabwe.
31. See, for example, Kenya, Anti-Corruption and Economic Crimes Act (ACECA), 2003, No. 3 of 2003, sec. 55.
32. For references to the laws that criminalize illicit enrichment, see, for example, United Nations Convention against Corruption. art. 20; Organization of American States (OAS), Inter-American Convention against Corruption (IACAC), art. IX; African Union Convention on Preventing and Combating Corruption (AUCPCC), art. 8; and Muzila et al. (2012), especially table 2.1 and appendix A, where over 40 jurisdictions are listed as having implemented an illicit enrichment offense.
33. See, for example, Kenya's Lifestyle Audit Bill, 2019, http://kenyalaw.org/kl/fileadmin /pdfdownloads/bills/2019/TheLifestyleAuditBill_2019.pdf.
34. United Kingdom, Proceeds of Crime Act, 2002, S.362B(6)(d).
35. See UK, National Crime Agency v. Baker et al., [2020] EWHC 822 (Admin) (April 8, 2020), at paras. 67, 86, 87, 140. In the UK case, a Global Witness report was one source used to initiate an investigation under the UK UWO. The case is currently being appealed.
36. See, for example, OECD (2016). On the other hand, whistleblower protections may also place certain restrictions on information sharing to the extent that the protections offered are not lost.
37. This option may be amended in the context of discussions related to modifications of FATF Recommendation 24.
38. See UK, Hajiyeva v. National Crime Agency, [2020] EWCA Civ 108 (February 5, 2020). The authorities relied, in part, on the appellant's declaration of beneficial ownership of a company, Vicksburg Global Inc., incorporated in the British Virgin Islands, which was registered as the sole proprietor of the property in which the appellant resided.
39. Coordination arrangements are established to ensure that policy making and implementation for related governance functions are carried out in line with a whole-of-government approach.
40. United Kingdom, Proceeds of Crime Act 2002, https://www.cps.gov.uk/publication /proceeds-crime-act-2002.
41. The terms *joint investigative team* and *joint task force* are used interchangeably unless otherwise specified.
42. OECD (2017a, 133). The countries include Australia, Austria, Azerbaijan, Brazil, Burkina Faso, Canada, the Czech Republic, Denmark, El Salvador, Finland, Germany, Ghana, Greece, Hungary, India, Israel, Japan, Luxembourg, Malaysia, the Netherlands, Portugal, Singapore, Slovenia, South Africa, Spain, Turkey, and the United States.
43. See, for example, the EU Model JIT Agreement, https://www.europol.europa.eu/publications -documents/model-agreement-for-setting-joint-investigation-team.
44. South Africa, Tax Administration Act, 2011, Act No. 28 of 2011, sec. 43-44, https://www.gov .za/sites/default/files/gcis_document/201409/a282011.pdf.
45. AUSTRAC, Fintel Alliance, https://www.austrac.gov.au/about-us/fintel-alliance.

46. AUSTRAC, Fintel Alliance, https://www.austrac.gov.au/about-us/fintel-alliance.
47. United Nations, About goAML, https://unite.un.org/goaml/content/approach-and-benefits. See also FSI (2019).
48. See Organisation for Economic Co-operation and Development, "OECD Releases IT-Tools to Support the Implementation of TRACE and the Wider Exchange of Tax Information," https://www.oecd.org/tax/exchange-of-tax-information/oecd-releases-it-tools-to-support-the-implementation-of-trace-and-the-wider-exchange-of-tax-information.htm; Organisation for Economic Co-operation and Development, "Automatic Exchange Portal: What Is the CRS?" https://www.oecd.org/tax/automatic-exchange/common-reporting-standard/.
49. Organisation for Economic Co-operation and Development, "Automatic Exchange Portal: Global Forum on Tax Transparency Marks a Dramatic Shift in the Right against Tax Evasion with the Widespread Commencement of the Automatic Exchange of Financial Information," https://www.oecd.org/tax/automatic-exchange/global-forum-marks-a-dramatic-shift-in-the-fight-against-tax-evasion-with-the-widespread-commencement-of-the-automatic-exchange-of-financial-information.htm.

References

ACIC (Australian Criminal Intelligence Commission). 2016. "ACIC Response to Panama Papers." Media release, September 6, 2016. https://www.acic.gov.au/media-centre/media-releases-and-statements/acic-response-panama-papers.

Bloomberg Tax. 2019. "INSIGHT: Mandatory Tax Disclosure Rules in EU—Confusion Galore." https://news.bloombergtax.com/daily-tax-report-international/insight-mandatory-tax-disclosure-rules-in-eu-confusion-galore.

Chenoweth, Neil, Fiona Buffini, and Hannah Low. 2011. "Behind the $430m Wickenby Saga." *Australian Financial Review*, Fairfax Media, May 3, 2011. https://www.afr.com/life-and-luxury/arts-and-culture/behind-the-430m-wickenby-saga-20110503-j4d7x.

Ching, Ooi Tee. 2019. *IRB Monitoring Social Media, Bank Accounts of Those with 'Unexplained Wealth.'* New Straits Times, January 14, 2019. https://www.nst.com.my/news/nation/2019/01/450526/irb-monitoring-social-media-bank-accounts-those-unexplained-wealth.

CNN. 2020. "He Flaunted Private Jets and Luxury Cars on Instagram. Feds Used His Posts to Link Him to Alleged Cyber Crimes." https://edition.cnn.com/2020/07/12/us/ray-hushpuppi-alleged-money-laundering-trnd/index.html.

Curran, Margaret. 2018. "OECD: Mandatory Disclosure Rules for Addressing CRS Avoidance Arrangements." *Tax Adviser*. https://www.taxadvisermagazine.com/article/oecd-mandatory-disclosure-rules-addressing-crs-avoidance-arrangements.

DW (Deutsche Welle). 2017. "German Investigators in Possession of Panama Papers, Aim to Prosecute Tax Cheats." July 7, 2017. https://www.dw.com/en/german-investigators-in-possession-of-panama-papers-aim-to-prosecute-tax-cheats/a-39547406.

ESAAMLG (Eastern and Southern Africa Anti-Money Laundering Group). 2017a. *First Round Mutual Evaluations: Post Evaluation Progress Report of Kenya.* Dar es Salaam, Tanzania: ESAAMLG. https://esaamlg.org/reports/Kenya%20R.pdf.

ESAAMLG (Eastern and Southern Africa Anti-Money Laundering Group). 2017b. *First Round Mutual Evaluations: Post Evaluation Progress Report of Zambia.* Dar es Salaam, Tanzania: ESAAMLG. https://esaamlg.org/reports/ZAMBIA%20R.pdf.

FATF (Financial Action Task Force). 2012a. *International Standards on Combating Money Laundering and the Financing of Terrorism and Proliferation: The FATF Recommendations.* Paris: FATF. https://www.fatf-gafi.org/media/fatf/documents/recommendations/pdfs/FATF%20Recommendations%202012.pdf.

FATF (Financial Action Task Force). 2012b. *Operational Issues: Financial Investigations Guidance.* Paris: FATF. http://www.fatf-gafi.org/media/fatf/documents/reports/Operational%20Issues_Financial%20investigations%20Guidance.pdf.

FATF (Financial Action Task Force). 2014. "Guidance on Transparency and Beneficial Ownership." Paris: FATF. http://www.fatf-gafi.org/media/fatf/documents/reports/Guidance-transparency-beneficial-ownership.pdf.

FATF (Financial Action Task Force). 2019. *Best Practices on Beneficial Ownership for Legal Persons.* Paris: FATF. http://www.fatf-gafi.org/media/fatf/documents/Best-Practices-Beneficial-Ownership-Legal-Persons.pdf.

FSI (Financial Stability Institute). 2019. "Suptech Applications for Anti-Money Laundering." FSI Insights on Policy Implementation No. 18. https://www.bis.org/fsi/publ/insights18.pdf.

GTPC (Global Tax Policy Center, Vienna University of Economics and Business). 2018. *Tax and Good Governance Project: Best Practices Manual.* Vienna: University of Economics and Business. https://www.wu.ac.at/fileadmin/wu/d/i/taxlaw/institute/WU_Global_Tax_Policy_Center/Siemens/Oct_2015/TGG_Electronic_Best_Practices_Manual_FINAL.pdf.

HMRC (Her Majesty's Revenue and Customs). 2019. "No Safe Havens 2019: Responding Appropriately." Policy paper, HMRC, London. https://www.gov.uk/government/publications/no-safe-havens-2019/no-safe-havens-2019-responding-appropriately.

IDB (Inter-American Development Bank) and OECD (Organisation for Economic Co-operation and Development). 2019. *A Beneficial Ownership Implementation Toolkit.* Prepared by Secretariat of the Global Forum of Transparency and Exchange of Information for Tax Purposes and IDB. Washington, DC: IDB. https://publications.iadb.org/publications/english/document/A_Beneficial_Ownership_Implementation_Toolkit_en_en.pdf.

IMF, Washington, DC. https://www.imf.org/external/np/pp/eng/2012/071712a.pdf.

ITR (International Tax Review). 2020. "Mexico: Mandatory Disclosure Requirements to Be Needed for Certain Tax Structures." https://www.internationaltaxreview.com/article/b1k9ccxz14xrpx/mexico-mandatory-disclosure-requirements-to-be-needed-for-certain-tax-structures.

Lötscher, Bernhard, and Axel Buhr. 2015. "Tax Fraud to Become Predicate Offence to Money Laundering." *International Law Office* (blog), August 31, 2015. https://www.internationallawoffice.com/Newsletters/White-Collar-Crime/Switzerland/CMS-von-Erlach-Poncet-Ltd/Tax-fraud-to-become-predicate-offence-to-money-laundering#Narrow%20definition%20of%20tax%20fraud.

Muzila, Lindy, Michelle Morales, Marianne Mathias, and Tammar Berger. 2012. *On the Take: Criminalizing Illicit Enrichment to Fight Corruption.* Stolen Asset Recovery Initiative

(StAR) of the World Bank and United Nations Office on Drugs and Crime. Washington, DC: World Bank.

NCA (National Crime Agency, United Kingdom). 2020. "Businessman with Links to Serious Criminals Loses Property Empire after Settling £10m Unexplained Wealth Order Case." https://www.wired-gov.net/wg/news.nsf/articles/Businessman+with+links+to+serious +criminals+loses+property+empire+after+settling+10m+Unexplained+Wealth+Order +case+08102020111500?open.

News18 (India). 2020. "Hotel Bills, Property Tax, School Fees to Now Reflect in ITR; All You Need to Know About I-T Form 26AS." August 14, 2020. https://www.news18.com/news /business/hotel-bills-property-tax-school-fees-to-now-reflect-in-itr-heres-all-you-need -to-know-about-income-tax-form-26as-2784583.html.

Nyaga, Caroline. No date. "Enhancing Synergies: The Multi-Agency Experience in Fighting Corruption in Kenya." 20th UNAFEI UNCAC Training Programme Participants' Paper and Resource Material Series No. 104. https://www.unafei.or.jp/publications/pdf/RS_No104 /No104_21_IP_Kenya.pdf.

Obonyo, Oscar. 2018. "Legal Hurdles Stand in Way of Lifestyle Audit." *Daily Nation*, June 30, 2018 (updated July 3, 2020). https://www.nation.co.ke/kenya/news/politics/-legal -hurdles-stand-in-way-of-lifestyle-audit-61510.

OECD (Organisation for Economic Co-operation and Development). 2012. *Keeping It Safe: The OECD Guide on the Protection of Confidentiality of Information Exchanged for Tax Purposes*. Paris: OECD Publishing.

OECD (Organisation for Economic Co-operation and Development). 2015a. *Improving Co-operation between Tax and Anti-Money Laundering Authorities: Access by Tax Administrations to Information Held by Financial Intelligence Units for Criminal and Civil Purposes*. Paris: OECD Publishing. https://www.oecd.org/ctp/crime/report-improving -cooperation-between-tax-anti-money-laundering-authorities.pdf.

OECD (Organisation for Economic Co-operation and Development). 2015b. *Mandatory Disclosure Rules, Action 12—2015 Final Report*. OECD/G20 Base Erosion and Profit Shifting Project. Paris: OECD Publishing.

OECD (Organisation for Economic Co-operation and Development). 2015c. *Model Protocol for the Purpose of Allowing the Automatic and Spontaneous Exchange of Information under a TIEA*. Paris: OECD Publishing. https://www.oecd.org/tax/exchange-of-tax -information/Model-Protocol-TIEA.pdf.

OECD (Organisation for Economic Co-operation and Development). 2016. *Committing to Effective Whistleblower Protection*. Paris: OECD Publishing. https://read.oecd-ilibrary .org/governance/committing-to-effective-whistleblower-protection_9789264252639 -en#page3.

OECD (Organisation for Economic Co-operation and Development). 2017a. *Effective Inter-Agency Cooperation in Fighting Tax Crime and Other Financial Crime,* 3d ed. Paris: OECD Publishing. https://www.oecd.org/tax/crime/effective-inter-agency-co-operation-in -fighting-tax-crimes-and-other-financial-crimes-third-edition.pdf.

OECD (Organisation for Economic Co-operation and Development). 2017b. *Fighting Tax Crime—The Ten Global Principles*. Paris: OECD Publishing. http://www.oecd.org/tax /crime/fighting-tax-crime-the-ten-global-principles.htm.

OECD (Organisation for Economic Co-operation and Development). 2018a. *Model Mandatory Disclosure Rules for CRS Avoidance Arrangements and Opaque Offshore Structures*. Paris:

OECD Publishing. https://www.oecd.org/tax/exchange-of-tax-information/model-mandatory-disclosure-rules-for-crs-avoidance-arrangements-and-opaque-offshore-structures.htm.

OECD (Organisation for Economic Co-operation and Development). 2018b. *The Framework for the Full AEOI Reviews: The Terms of Reference.* Global Forum on Transparency and Exchange of Information for Tax Purposes. Paris: OECD Publishing. https://www.oecd.org/tax/transparency/AEOI-terms-of-reference.pdf.

OECD (Organisation for Economic Co-operation and Development). 2020. *Tax Crime Investigation Maturity Model*. Paris: OECD Publishing. http://www.oecd.org/tax/crime/tax-crime-investigation-maturity-model.htm.

OECD (Organisation for Economic Co-operation and Development) and World Bank. 2018. *Improving Co-operation between Tax Authorities and Anti-Corruption Authorities in Combating Tax Crime and Corruption*. Paris: OECD Publishing.

Palin, Adam. 2016. "HMRC Prosecutions Unlikely after Panama Papers Leak." *Financial Times*, April 13, 2016. https://www.ft.com/content/a277646c-0091-11e6-ac98-3c15a1aa2e62.

Riondet, Simon. 2018. "The Value of Public-Private Partnerships for Financial Intelligence." *Journal of Financial Compliance* 2 (2): 148–54. https://hstalks.com/article/4944/the-value-of-public-private-partnerships-for-finan/.

Schlenther, Bernd. 2017. "Tax Administrations, Financial Intelligence Units, Law Enforcement Agencies: How to Work Together?" In *Inter-agency Cooperation and Good Tax Governance in Africa*, edited by Jeffrey Owens, Rick McDonell, Riël Franzsen, and Jude Amos. Pretoria, South Africa: Pretoria University Law Press.

Smyth, Jamie. 2019. "Glencore Loses 'Paradise Papers' Court Case in Australia." *Financial Times*, August 14, 2019. https://www.ft.com/content/c702ceea-be55-11e9-b350-db00d509634e.

Somare, Maryte. 2017. "The Increasing Use of the Beneficial Ownership Concept from the Anti-Money Laundering Framework in Furthering the Tax Transparency Agenda." In *Inter-Agency Cooperation and Good Tax Governance in Africa*, edited by Jeffrey Owens, Rick McDonell, Riël Franzsen, and Jude Amos. Pretoria, South Africa: Pretoria University Law Press.

SwissInfo. 2019. "Switzerland Rejects German Panama Papers Offer." January 27, 2019. https://www.swissinfo.ch/eng/legal-restrictions_switzerland-rejects-german-panama-papers-offer/44712630.

TFI Info. 2020. "Data-Mining, Artificial Intelligence at the Service of the Tax Authorities." July 2, 2020. https://www.lci.fr/high-tech/comment-l-intelligence-artificielle-du-fisc-traque-les-fraudeurs-en-ligne-fraude-fiscale-gerald-darmanin-bercy-milliards-2137176.html.

Transparency International. 2017. "Obiang Verdict: Transparency International Welcomes the Corruption Conviction and Seizure of Assets." https://www.transparency.org/en/press/obiang-verdict-transparency-international-welcomes-the-corruption-convictio (last accessed 9 July 2020).

Unger, Brigitte. 2017. "Money Laundering and Tax Evasion." Coffers EU Horizon 2020 Project, Utrecht University, Utrecht, the Netherlands. http://coffers.eu/wp-content/uploads/2019/11/D6.2-Working-Paper.pdf.

Unger, Brigitte, Joras Ferwerda, Lucia Flores Russel, and Andoni Montes. 2018. "Money Laundering and Tax Fraud." Coffers EU Horizon 2020 Project, Utrecht University, Utrecht, the Netherlands. http://coffers.eu/wp-content/uploads/2019/11/D6.4-Working-Paper.pdf.

US Department of Justice. 2018. "Four Defendants Charged in Panama Papers Investigations for their Roles in Panamanian-Based Global Law Firm's Decades-Long Scheme to Defraud the United States." Press release, Office of Public Affairs, December 4, 2018. https://www.justice.gov/opa/pr/four-defendants-charged-panama-papers -investigation-their-roles-panamanian-based-global-law.

3. Combining Tax and Financial Crime Prosecution in an Interagency Asset Recovery Strategy

3.1 Introduction

Proper implementation of the tools and information sharing methods identified in chapter 2 to enhance interagency cooperation generally pays off because it often allows prosecutors to leverage tax evasion charges to fight corruption or money laundering and, conversely, to use money laundering charges to go after tax evasion schemes. It can also lead to the simultaneous pursuit of tax evasion and money laundering charges.

In the prosecution of a financial crime, interagency cooperation will be highly dependent on a country's institutional framework. Although multiple agencies are typically involved in the prosecution of corruption, money laundering, and tax crimes, the law may provide only selected agencies with the authority to initiate prosecution. Options include the following:

- Some tax authorities have access to specialized tax tribunals with a mandate to decide on the correctness of a tax assessment but do not have the power to prosecute tax crimes and impose criminal sentences. Appeals on the decisions made by these tribunals are heard in national courts. For example, the Tax Appeals Tribunal in Zambia deals with taxpayer objections to tax authority assessments, which is a civil tax litigation process.
- Prosecution authorities or an investigative magistrate represent the state in court for the prosecution of all criminal offenses (OECD and World Bank 2018).
- In some countries, law enforcement agencies (LEAs), including anticorruption authorities, may directly prosecute a crime (OECD and World Bank 2018). For example, in Nigeria, the Independent Corrupt Practices and Other Related Offences Commission (ICPC) and the Economic and Financial Crimes Commission (EFCC) are empowered to prosecute corruption offenses (OECD and World Bank 2018).
- The attorney general may help LEAs initiate prosecution of a case.

Regardless of how prosecution is initiated, the agencies or units involved will have specialized knowledge and skills. Interagency teams can benefit from this specialization and avoid any potential duplication of efforts. Where more than one agency is empowered to prosecute the same types of offenses, clear guidelines will be important in determining when and how each agency will intervene. Interagency cooperation can ensure that these agencies combine efforts, exchange evidence, and use the unique procedures available.

One major benefit of increased cooperation between tax authorities and LEAs is the ability to initiate simultaneous prosecution via the national courts and specialized tax tribunals, thereby increasing the chances of success. Simultaneous prosecution can prevent suspects from evading authorities (or limit their ability to do so) and increase the likelihood of recovery of at least some of the assets. Conversely, consecutive prosecutions are more likely to fail as evidence grows stale or suspects flee or die.

A joint approach allows authorities to determine whether the evidence obtained "more clearly indicates one type of crime over another" and then to "set the case strategy appropriately" (OECD and World Bank 2018, 79). Joint teams can better handle evidence (in accordance with the rules of procedure) and ensure that a suspect's rights and protections are safeguarded throughout the process. Tax information can act as the starting point of an investigation, but it is often not admissible as evidence in a corruption or money laundering prosecution unless it is obtained using specific procedures. In addition, although tax information, details of assets, bank accounts, or other financial transactions can be assumed to be reliable at face value, other documents may require validation or verification prior to criminal prosecution.

3.2 Prosecuting Tax Evasion to Fight Organized or Financial Crime

Organized crime offenses, corruption, embezzlement, money laundering, and other crimes may be challenging to prove, depending on the evidence collected. Sometimes, prosecutors drop a case if acquittal becomes a possibility for lack of evidence. In this situation, also charging the defendant with tax offenses may preserve a path to criminal conviction because often countries criminalize possession of undeclared revenue or assets.

In the prosecution of organized crime, the practice of charging defendants with a tax crime has been well established for almost a century. In 1927, the US Supreme Court ruled in *United States v. Sullivan* that illegally earned income was subject to income tax, and on June 16, 1931, Chicago gangster Al Capone famously pled guilty to tax evasion and eventually was sentenced to prison for 11 years. Criminal investigators should consider, then, charging defendants with tax offenses, in addition to organized crime, corruption, or other applicable white-collar offenses.

In large, complex financial investigations, interagency teams may manage the prosecution process (FATF 2012). It is particularly important for prosecutors who draw on the expertise of officials from other LEAs to profit from that expertise to present the case in court more effectively (FATF 2012). Generally, countries have mixed approaches to sharing information with public prosecutors. The approaches vary—direct access, requirements to report, the ability to share with discretion, and sharing on request (OECD 2017a). See box 3.1 for country examples.

Some jurisdictions also have expanded their reach to target tax collection from certain offshore arrangements. The range of information that tax authorities can obtain from or about taxpayers engaged in complex offshore arrangements and their ability to pursue these individuals for potential tax crimes also create opportunities for the investigation and recovery of the proceeds of money laundering and other financial crimes—they are often found within these complex offshore arrangements.

BOX 3.1   **Country Examples of Information Sharing between Tax Authorities and Prosecutors**

The 2017 report by the Organisation for Economic Co-operation and Development on effective interagency cooperation identified various approaches to information sharing with a prosecutor's office (OECD 2017a). These include:

- *Direct access to relevant databases.* In Chile, the tax authority established a secure website through which the public prosecutor's office can directly access tax information. In Estonia, tax authorities and the police share a common intelligence database, accessible by both.

- *Direct access through joint investigative task forces.* In Spain, direct access to information is possible when tax authorities are part of an investigation. When they are not, the public prosecutor or examining judge may request the information. In Australia, the Australian Serious Financial Crime Taskforce (SFCT) was established in 2015 as an Australian Tax Office–led interagency task force to deal with the most serious and complex forms of financial crime. The SFCT includes the police, the financial intelligence unit, and the prosecutor's office, among other agencies, thereby facilitating information sharing.

- *Spontaneous information sharing.* In the Czech Republic, tax authorities are required to report to the public prosecutor any suspected offenses and spontaneously provide information relevant to a reported offense. In any other circumstances, the prosecutor may request information from the tax administration.

3.3 Prosecuting Money Laundering and Corruption to Fight Tax Evasion

Where tax crimes have been recognized as a predicate offense to money laundering, a person charged with a tax offense can also be charged with money laundering. Any prosecution is dependent on the nature of the evidence obtained and the elements of the offense to be proven (OECD 2017b). Jurisdictions that recognize tax crimes as a predicate offense for money laundering, as per the Financial Action Task Force (FATF) recommendations, report that doing so enhances their ability to undertake money laundering prosecutions, increases the number of successful prosecutions, and has a deterrent effect on would-be offenders (OECD 2017b).

In advocating the need to expand the scope of money laundering predicate offenses to include tax crimes, the FATF recognized that the anti-money laundering (AML) framework could prove useful in complementing and supporting tax authorities combating tax crimes. The inclusion of tax crimes is particularly important because authorities have a wider scope to secure a conviction or impose a penalty, and avenues for international cooperation under the FATF recommendations are expanded to include tax authorities (OECD 2017b). The latter includes access to the direct exchange of information and mutual legal assistance (MLA) between tax authorities and prosecution authorities (OECD 2017b).

Many jurisdictions have enacted legislation reversing the burden of proof in corruption, money laundering, or organized crime cases by using notions such as illicit enrichment, unjustified resources, or "lifestyle" audits, as described in chapter 2, section 2.4.1.4. In some cases, the consequences may be criminal and include imprisonment, confiscation, and fines (such as for "illicit enrichment offences"[1]), while in others the consequences are civil (such as for nonconviction-based recovery of assets and monetary sanctions).[2] These laws reflect the view that corruption or white-collar crime prosecutions justify the use of powerful legal presumptions, leaving it up to defendants to prove that the statutory presumption does not apply to their case.

In this context, investigating discrepancies between legitimate income and assets held and using these legal tools can result in the confiscation or the recovery of assets undeclared in the jurisdiction of the defendant. A similar result may be achieved from a tax proceeding, but that differs in that it is extended to also capture nontax crimes. If the assets are in a jurisdiction other than that in which the case is initiated, enforcement may require that similar illicit enrichment criminal offenses take place in both jurisdictions. See box 3.2 for country examples of tools based on illicit enrichment or possession of unjustified resources in specific circumstances.

Beyond the legislation on unexplained wealth, adding money laundering charges to the prosecution of suspected financial fraud or tax evasion often opens opportunities to extend the case to the recovery of unpaid taxes or undeclared revenue. In these situations, recovery of the proceeds of tax evasion benefits from the tools used by public prosecutors or investigating magistrates.

BOX 3.2	Country Examples of Illicit Enrichment and Possession of Unjustified Resources

France. In 2013, France enacted a reform on money laundering. When financial transactions obviously have no purpose other than concealing the origin of funds or the ownership of assets, these funds or assets can be confiscated as proceeds or instruments of money laundering, unless the defendant proves the legitimate origin of the funds or assets. In addition, for all predicate offenses punishable by at least five years of imprisonment, the confiscation can be carried out for all the properties of the defendant, unless the defendant proves that their origin is legitimate. Some have called into question the constitutionality of these provisions, but the French Supreme Court determined they were constitutional in its decision of June 16, 1999. Similarly, in its decision of October 7, 1988, the European Court of Human Rights found that, under certain circumstances, presumptions of law or facts are acceptable in criminal law if the burden on the defendant is not excessive or disproportionate. As a result, French prosecutors can now open investigations on the laundering of proceeds derived from tax evasion, which allows the use of anti-money laundering and organized crime procedural tools.

Mauritius. Mauritius introduced the concept of the unexplained wealth order (UWO) in the Good Governance and Integrity Reporting Act 2015 (GGIRA), which also established the Integrity Reporting Services Agency (IRSA). The GGIRA applies to the property of Mauritian citizens, regardless of location. Under this statute, a UWO is a form of nonconviction-based asset confiscation (action *in rem*) and does not require a criminal conviction. The GGIRA also shifts the burden of proof to the owner of the property, who must show, on the balance of probabilities, that his or her wealth is of legitimate origin.

The first UWO granted in Mauritius was obtained when the Mauritius Revenue Authority (MRA) referred a case to the IRSA of a man stopped at the airport carrying a huge amount of undeclared cash. Had the MRA believed the cash to be of legitimate origin, it would have raised a tax assessment and applied a penalty. However, in this case the MRA did not believe it to be of legitimate origin and so referred the matter to the IRSA. The man similarly failed to show the IRSA and a high court judge that, on the balance of probabilities, the cash had a legitimate source, and so it was confiscated through a UWO.

A good example of information flows in the other direction occurred when the IRSA referred a case to the MRA. The respondent in question was suspected of involvement in money laundering by converting proceeds of drug offenses into immoveable property and a variety of businesses. In seeking to demonstrate the legitimate origin of his assets, his salary slips showed the respondent was not filing his tax returns properly. They were then turned over to the MRA, which initiated a tax assessment and then applied a penalty. The referral to the MRA had no impact on the IRSA's unexplained wealth investigation, which is ongoing.

Prosecutors who launch money laundering investigations often consider also charging tax evasion for two reasons: (1) the nondisclosure of assets in foreign jurisdictions is frequently a tax violation per se; and (2) the undeclared foreign assets may be derived from the proceeds of tax fraud, and, if so, their transfer or possession abroad constitutes laundering of the proceeds of criminal tax evasion. Because criminal investigators or prosecutors are often authorized, and sometimes obliged, by law to disclose potential tax violations to tax authorities, this information will enable tax authorities to enforce their mandate.

As emphasized in chapter 2, anticorruption authorities, financial intelligence units (FIUs), or police investigating nontax offenses may obtain information relevant to an ongoing tax investigation or that identifies a potential tax crime. In 2017, a review conducted of 50 jurisdictions by the Organisation for Economic Co-operation and Development (OECD) established that most countries provided gateways enabling police and public prosecutors to share information with tax authorities or for direct access (OECD 2017b). Successful prosecution of tax offenses or recovery of taxes can be the result of information or evidence collected by criminal investigators, as seen in high-profile cases 7 and 8 in the appendix, and some countries have specific arrangements that promote this type of coordination—see box 3.3 for a country example.

Charging a defendant with money laundering when tax fraud is possibly the source of the laundered assets has another advantage in that it may help detect and prove the role of facilitators who help construct complex transactions, arrange the seemingly legitimate investment of illicit funds, and exploit tax havens and jurisdictions with weak anti-money laundering regimes (Blackham 2017).

Choosing to bring a money laundering charge allows the use of specific investigative measures authorized by prosecutors or judges in the context of organized crime cases. Reliance on these measures, including wiretapping, electronic surveillance, proactive searches and seizures, and undercover operations, may be more challenging and sometimes impossible for both legal and practical reasons in the absence of money laundering charges and in cases of less serious incriminations.

BOX 3.3	When Tax Authorities Benefit from the Input of Criminal Investigators and Prosecutors

In Kenya, criminal tax investigations are carried out in a hybrid system whereby the tax audit investigators work jointly with police officers attached to the tax authority. The charges are prepared with technical input from tax auditors, internal tax investigators, and in-house lawyers. Concurrence is obtained from the director of public prosecutions on tax offenses before the police undertake the final arrest and arraignment in court. In other cases, the tax authority receives evidence collected by other agencies such as the anticorruption agency, financial intelligence unit, and asset recovery agency, among others, under the Multi-Agency Taskforce framework. This way, the tax authority takes full advantage of the input of criminal investigators and prosecutors.

Such investigative techniques often lead to uncovering information, documentation, and evidence involving the enablers who provided the main defendant with technical advice. Enablers could include financial institutions, lawyers, accountants, trust and company service providers, and real estate agents. Expanding investigations and prosecutions to cover these enablers is key to successful prosecution because these defendants are often tempted to cooperate with authorities and provide evidence against the main defendants in return for fewer or less serious charges and sentences. This factor may prove invaluable in cases in which prosecutors need to convince judges (and sometimes jurors) of the accuracy and seriousness of the facts.

Recovering proceeds from enablers and other professionals may also be an effective asset recovery option for authorities. In particular, facilitators with deep pockets, such as banks, that risk criminal prosecution based on the role they played in money laundering schemes may prefer to cooperate with authorities and pay large sums in settlements or deferred prosecution agreements.[3] Such an arrangement could also deter professionals from playing a role in facilitating the hiding of illicit wealth and assets.

3.4 Pursuing Tax Offenses in Parallel with Money Laundering

As indicated in chapter 2, tax crimes and money laundering cases often involve individuals or companies that have large undeclared estates or assets (including bank accounts) in tax havens or in countries with lax tax regimes, or that create fake documents to justify the origin of foreign assets. Following an extensive investigation, authorities are often able to map the complex structures through which an individual may be holding and hiding assets, perhaps across several jurisdictions and through a variety of legal vehicles. As a result, prosecutors aiming to recover the proceeds of a crime will need to make strategic decisions to maximize the chances of successful asset recovery.

There are many potential benefits to prosecuting money laundering and tax offenses in parallel, even though extra resources may be required. At a minimum, this choice will allow the tax administration to tax the undeclared income and recover penalties in parallel administrative tax proceedings (see case 2 in the appendix) while the criminal prosecution follows its course. In some jurisdictions such as France, criminal prosecutors can charge the defendant with tax evasion in addition to money laundering, and tax authorities can claim restitution of unpaid taxes during the criminal trial. In some jurisdictions, the same agency may be tasked with conducting both avenues. See box 3.4 for country examples.

BOX 3.4	Agencies Pursuing Both Tax Evasion and Money Laundering

Ireland, Criminal Assets Bureau. Recognizing the benefits of pursuing both recovery of the proceeds of a crime and recovery of unpaid taxes, Ireland established and equipped its Criminal Assets Bureau (CAB) with the powers to do just that.[a] CAB combines seizure, tax, and recovery powers. It is composed of officers from An Garda Síochána (Ireland's National Police and Security Service), Revenue Commissioners, and Department of Employment Affairs and Social Protection. In some years, the amounts recovered under the revenue provisions (taxes, interest, and so forth) exceed those recovered under the proceeds of crime legislation.[b]

Table B3.4.1 Recovered Funds, Criminal Assets Bureau, Ireland, 2015–18

Year	Proceeds of crime legislation (€, millions)	Revenue provisions (€, millions)	Social welfare provisions (€)
2015	>2.2	>2.2	323,000
2016	>1.6	>2.3	319,000
2017	>1.4	>2	297,430
2018	>1.6	>2	185,354

Source: Criminal Assets Bureau, Ireland, Annual Reports, 2015–18, https://www.cab.ie/annual-reports/.

United Kingdom, National Crime Agency's revenue powers. Through the Proceeds of Crime Act, the United Kingdom has granted certain "revenue" powers to the National Crime Agency (NCA) so it can pursue both asset recovery and taxation in parallel. In addition to granting the NCA powers to recover assets or property that it can prove, on the balance of probability, have been acquired through unlawful conduct, any profits derived from these assets can also be recovered. The NCA recognizes that taxation can be "a particularly powerful tool for recovering criminal assets." It initiates tax assessments and pursues tax liability as well as penalties and interest whenever it has reasonable grounds to suspect the income or assets are illicit.[c]

a. Ireland, Criminal Assets Bureau Act, 1996. See also Criminal Assets Bureau, https://www.cab.ie/.
b. Ireland, Criminal Assets Bureau, Annual Reports, 2015–18, https://www.cab.ie/annual-reports/.
c. United Kingdom, National Crime Agency, https://nationalcrimeagency.gov.uk/what-we-do/how-we-work/providing-specialist-capabilities-for-law-enforcement/civil-recovery-and-tax.

Notes

1. Modeled on the United Nations Convention against Corruption (UNCAC), art. 20; Inter-American Convention against Corruption (IACAC), art. IX; and African Union Convention on Preventing and Combating Corruption (AUCPCC), art. 8.

2. For example, in South Africa the civil recovery of property under Chapter 6 of the Prevention of Organized Crime Act, 1998.
3. In the 1Malaysia Development Berhad (1MDB) case, for example, Malaysia recovered $2.9 billion from Goldman Sachs in a settlement linked to the embezzlement of money diverted from its sovereign fund. See US Department of Justice (2020).

References

Blackham, Anthony. 2017. "Why Lawyers Are a Crucial Line of Defence for Tackling Money Laundering." *Telegraph,* February 10, 2017. http://www.telegraph.co.uk/money/criminal -activities/anti-money-laundering-solicitors-front-line-defence/.

FATF (Financial Action Task Force). 2012. *Operational Issues: Financial Investigations Guidance.* Paris: FATF. http://www.fatf-gafi.org/media/fatf/documents/reports /Operational%20Issues_Financial%20investigations%20Guidance.pdf.

OECD (Organisation for Economic Co-operation and Development). 2017a. *Effective Inter-Agency Cooperation in Fighting Tax Crime and Other Financial Crimes.* 3d ed. Paris: OECD Publishing. https://www.oecd.org/tax/crime/effective-inter-agency-co-operation -in-fighting-tax-crimes-and-other-financial-crimes-third-edition.pdf.

OECD (Organisation for Economic Co-operation and Development). 2017b. *Fighting Tax Crime—The Ten Global Principles.* http://www.oecd.org/tax/crime/fighting-tax-crime -the-ten-global-principles.htm.

OECD (Organisation for Economic Co-operation and Development) and World Bank. 2018. *Improving Co-operation between Tax Authorities and Anti-Corruption Authorities in Combating Tax Crime and Corruption.* Paris: OECD Publishing.

US Department of Justice. 2020. "Goldman Sachs Resolves Foreign Bribery Case and Agrees to Pay Over $2.9 Billion." Press release, October 22, 2020. https://www.justice .gov/usao->edny/pr/goldman-sachs-resolves-foreign-bribery-case-and-agrees-pay -over-29-billion.

4. Developing Interagency Exchanges of Information at the Regional and International Levels

4.1 Introduction

Large-scale international corruption, money laundering, and tax evasion have a cross-border component requiring investigators and prosecutors to use all available channels to exchange information with and obtain evidence from foreign jurisdictions. The scope for international cooperation is wide. It could involve formal and informal cooperation in exchanging information (such as that on beneficial ownership of legal entities, arrangements, or bank accounts), acting on behalf of foreign counterparts (such as arresting individuals, freezing or confiscating assets, or using investigative techniques to obtain information), or setting up joint task forces, whereby authorities collaborate and perform their respective scopes of action. Models for formal and informal cooperation are described in chapter 2, section 2.5.

Both international legal and administrative frameworks have expanded to enable collaboration across jurisdictions, which, in turn, has improved national cooperation efforts. First, these frameworks have provided for formal channels of communication to enable the collection of evidence, cooperation in investigations and prosecutions, as well as a formal process for asset recovery from foreign jurisdictions. Second, the frameworks have encouraged more interactions and dialogue between a variety of agencies in different countries, notably through international forums. Finally, because of this dialogue and the rapport established between agencies, informal communication channels have emerged that increase the efficiency of formal communications by, for example, helping in the preparation of formal requests.

Meanwhile, the informal channels provided by international forums have proved to be enormously important for interagency cooperation at the international level, where agencies with different functionalities and in different countries have had an opportunity to interact directly. When tax authorities and law enforcement agencies (LEAs) join forces in special investigative units at the domestic level, these units may be able to combine the channels for informal and formal exchange of information available to each agency, facilitating access of the special investigative units to international cooperation.

4.2 Using Tax Transparency Instruments in Prosecuting Money Laundering and Corruption

4.2.1 Overview of the Main Tax Transparency Instruments

Effective exchange of information and overall tax transparency are essential to combat tax crimes. Since publication of the 1998 Organisation for Economic Co-operation and Development (OECD) report *Harmful Tax Competition* (OECD 1998), efforts to address the role of secrecy in facilitating tax crimes have culminated in the development of Exchange of Information on Request (EOIR) and Automatic Exchange of Information (AEOI) standards. The implementation of these standards by countries is reviewed and monitored by the Global Forum on Transparency and Exchange of Information for Tax Purposes, with the support of the OECD. The standards on EOIR are implemented through bilateral tax treaties, tax information exchange agreements (TIEAs),[1] and the Multilateral Convention on Mutual Administrative Assistance in Tax Matters (MCMA).[2] The standard on AEOI is implemented through the Common Reporting Standards Multilateral Competent Authority Agreement (CRS MCAA).[3] Competent Authority Agreements (CAAs)[4] can be used for either EOIR or AEOI purposes.

Countries often conclude bilateral tax treaties to eliminate double taxation, allocate taxing rights, prevent the avoidance or evasion of taxes, and facilitate the exchange of information between tax authorities. Article 26 of both the OECD Model Tax Convention and the UN Model Tax Convention governs exchange of information between competent tax authorities to enable administration or enforcement of domestic tax laws. It can be either on request, spontaneous, or automatic, as described shortly. This information is not limited to taxpayer-specific information and can include other sensitive information related to tax administration and compliance improvement.[5]

The MCMA, drafted in 1988 by the OECD and the Council of Europe and revised in 2010, is a multilateral agreement to promote international cooperation between countries in the assessment and collection of taxes with a view toward combating tax avoidance and evasion. With 137 participating jurisdictions, it is used as an instrument for all forms of tax cooperation. The MCMA provides for all forms of mutual assistance, including simultaneous tax examinations, tax examinations abroad, exchange of information (in all forms), service of documents, and assistance in recovery of taxes. Article 26 of the OECD Model Tax Convention (MTC) and the MCMA provide the basis for all forms of information exchange (OECD 2014).

The CRS MCAA is a multilateral instrument that facilitates AEOI. It sets out the financial account information to be exchanged, the financial institutions required to report, the types of accounts and individuals or entities covered, as well as the common due diligence procedures to be followed by financial institutions. The aim is to create a global network of exchange that would allow financial information to flow back and forth between countries regularly. Over 100 jurisdictions have committed to implementing the CRS, and all financial centers have been called to match those commitments. Countries may also bilaterally engage in AEOI through CAAs designed to achieve the same outcome.

These international agreements generally provide three types of exchange of information assistance:

- *On request.* The standards for effective EOIR originate from the OECD's Model Agreement on Exchange of Information on Tax Matters (Model TIEA) 2002 and Article 26 of the MTC and its commentary. The competent tax authority is required to provide information that is foreseeably relevant (that is, necessary or may be relevant) upon request. This includes both information held by banks and other financial institutions or persons acting in a fiduciary capacity (nominees or trustees) and information identifying the beneficial owner of a legal person, legal arrangement, or bank account. EOIR is also provided under Article 5, Chapter III, of the MCMA. Under this framework, the requested state should provide foreseeably relevant information for the requesting state's administration or enforcers of its domestic laws concerning the particular person or transaction.
- *Spontaneous.* This type of agreement entails the provision of information that is foreseeably relevant to another contracting state that was not previously requested. It relies on the active participation and cooperation of tax authorities, and its effectiveness is highly reliant on their efficiency. Spontaneous exchanges are guided by Article 26 of the MTC and the MCMA. They may involve information about the beneficial owner of a legal person, legal arrangement, or bank account, including one held by a financial institution or persons acting in accord with their fiduciary duty.
- *Automatic.* The AEOI provided for under the OECD's Common Reporting Standard and designed to address tax evasion as well as improve tax compliance involves the automatic transmission of financial account information between tax authorities. This type of transmission enables countries to receive information about offshore accounts without showing whether the information is "foreseeably relevant." Participating countries in the CRS MCAA exchange pre-agreed-on categories of information annually without the need for a request.

Moreover, unlike traditional mutual legal assistance in which the requesting jurisdiction must adhere to the "standard of proof" in the requested jurisdiction in order to seek information, the MTC and MCMA prescribe that information be provided where it is "foreseeably relevant." Commentary on Article 26 of the MTC further clarifies that where such a showing is made, the request shall not be declined on the basis that a higher standard of proof must be met.

4.2.2 Use of Tax Transparency Instruments in Money Laundering Investigations

Although the objective of the just-described methods of exchange of information is to promote international cooperation in tax matters, the broad access granted to tax authorities may be useful not only in detecting tax crimes, but also in identifying potential money laundering, corruption, or bribery. Because of the nature of financial crimes, the same activity may violate a number of different laws. Tax crimes are "intrinsically linked to other financial crimes as criminals fail to report their income from illicit activities for tax purposes" or they may "over report income in an attempt to launder the proceeds of crime" (OECD 2013, 7). For example, in the case of a Middle Eastern financial institution, a country submitted a TIEA request and tax treaty request for any activities related to undeclared accounts with this institution, and the information gained led to criminal prosecution. The financial institution paid $270 million in fines and penalties and had to turn over the names of 1,500 US account holders.

Initially, the commentary on Article 26 of the OECD MTC provided that mutual assistance between tax authorities could only be possible for tax offenses and if each administration was assured that the information would be treated with proper secrecy (OECD 2012). Thus, crucially, the condition that attached to any information was that it could only be used for tax purposes. Later, the OECD proposed to include in the commentary on Article 26 a provision permitting the sharing of tax information by tax authorities with other LEAs and judicial authorities and for certain nontax purposes on high-priority issues, including money laundering and corruption. In 2012, the text extended the capacity to engage in information sharing with relevant LEAs when tax authorities obtain information on request (from an EOIR), through a spontaneous exchange of information, or automatically (an AEOI)—see OECD (2012).

4.2.3 Use of Transparency Tax Instruments in International Joint Investigation Teams

In addition to the sources of information just described, information can also be exchanged internationally through the establishment of joint investigation teams (JITs). JITs that are limited in scope and that aim at "capitalizing on each participating authority's particular expertise" can give rise to significant benefits (OECD 2017a, 25). JITs are an efficient way of ensuring the direct and instantaneous exchange of information between investigators and prosecutors from different jurisdictions.

The possibility of setting up JITs between Member States of the European Union (EU) appears in Article 13 of the 2000 EU Mutual Legal Assistance Convention. In view of the slow progress toward its ratification, on June 13, 2002, the European Council adopted the Framework Decision on JITs (Eurojust 2002), which Member States began to implement in 2004. These instruments have provided for two particular situations in which a JIT can be established:

- In demanding cross-border investigations—that is, when a Member State's investigations into criminal offenses require complex, demanding investigations having links with other Member States.
- In connected investigations requiring coordination—that is, when a number of Member States are conducting investigations into criminal offenses in which the circumstances of the case require coordinated, concerted action in the Member States involved.

The Missing Stone Trader case is an example of such a transnational investigation of tax fraud. This case, which involved a value added tax (VAT) carousel, elicited a high degree of national cooperation to audit suspected companies and international cooperation between police and tax authorities in three countries to examine payments and invoices and to verify the transport for sale of stone from country 1 to country 2 (see case 3 in the appendix). Uncovered in 2013, the scheme incurred €27.5 million in lost VAT revenue for both countries. The case included the collection of data on 67 front companies, the interception of communications between perpetrators, covert surveillance, and various tracking technologies. Overall, 29 searches were conducted of businesses and private residences to seize documents, records, and computers.

As the Missing Stone Trader case demonstrates, JITs can be beneficial in investigating cases of tax fraud and can include tax auditors. As explained in the practical guide drawn up by Europol,[6] contributions from persons who are neither law enforcement nor judicial authorities are often beneficial to the outcome of an investigation. When seconded, JIT members not from LEAs, including agents from tax authorities, may be entrusted by the JIT leader of the country in which the team operates to carry out investigative measures.

4.3 Using Anti-Money Laundering Tools to Pursue International Tax Evasion

4.3.1 Overview

When law enforcement agencies launch a money laundering investigation involving assets or transactions in another jurisdiction, they often request informal assistance and mutual legal assistance (MLA) in criminal matters in seeking information or evidence, help with the extradition of a suspect, or overall support in freezing or seizing assets. This information can also be highly relevant to authorities tackling tax evasion (IMF 2012). If a crime is identified as a predicate offense to money laundering, the offender may be investigated for both the original crime and for money laundering (IMF 2012). When considering whether to include tax crimes as predicate offenses, the Financial Action Task Force (FATF) surveyed the national legislation adopted by a number of OECD countries to determine their experience in using the anti-money laundering (AML) framework to combat tax crimes and identify the extent to which the existing standards already covered tax offenses (IMF 2012). Consultations with stakeholders revealed that the FATF needed to address the growing threat of the laundering of proceeds of tax crimes (FATF 2011).

4.3.2 Use of Informal International Cooperation in Criminal and Tax Matters

Mutual legal assistance is typically a very lengthy, complex process. Certainly, when initiating a case, investigators prefer to use less formal and less restrictive ways of obtaining the information they need to develop their investigation. Although acquiring evidence that will be used in court (such as witness statements and documents found during searches and seizures) generally requires MLA and cannot be obtained in any other way, information and documents useful to developing investigations can be exchanged through less formal processes—such as from one financial intelligence unit (FIU) to another and police to police. Exchanges of information via tax information agencies, when possible, may also be a useful way to gather information. Such channels may or may not be accepted, depending on domestic legislation and the treaties applicable in the jurisdictions involved.

The connection between tax authorities and other LEAs can also benefit from international networks and forums. For example, international cooperation in criminal cases in the context of asset recovery efforts can be conducted through the Camden Asset Recovery Inter-agency Network (CARIN). CARIN is an informal network of law enforcement and judicial practitioners engaged in asset tracing, freezing, seizure, and confiscation in 54 registered member jurisdictions.[7] The representatives of the member states are called "national contact points." Although certain cross-border actions (such as enforcing confiscation orders) require formal channels of cooperation, national contact points can exchange operational information to *support* the complete asset recovery process, from the starting point of the investigation involving the tracing of assets to freezing and seizure, management, and finally forfeiture/confiscation, including any necessary asset sharing between jurisdictions.

CARIN focuses on recovering the proceeds of crime, which can involve criminal investigations of money laundering of the proceeds of tax fraud or tax evasion. It is also linked to the six other regional asset recovery interagency networks (ARINs) across the world.[8] The exchange of key information or evidence in criminal cases (such as beneficial ownership of assets or companies and location of assets, among other things) can lead to discoveries of tax fraud or tax evasion. In such cases, the country receiving such information may decide to open a tax evasion investigation in addition to the criminal proceedings it was initially conducting. The information could also be transferred to tax auditors for the purpose of routine tax verifications.

For FIUs, similar exchanges of information through the Egmont Group can be considered as well. Egmont is a network of 167 FIUs devoted to "secure exchanges of expertise and financial intelligence to combat money laundering and terrorist financing."[9] It provides a forum in which FIUs can engage in information exchange, identify any barriers to exchange and address them, and develop new partnerships. Again, information related to money laundering investigations may provide the receiving jurisdictions with the key elements of a possible tax fraud case or verification points in a tax audit.

At the regional level, the European Union has witnessed significant developments in channels and tools that enable cross-border interagency cooperation and coordination (see box 4.1 for notable examples of coordination mechanisms within the European Union).

BOX 4.1	Regional Cooperation Mechanisms within EU Member States

European Union Agency for Criminal Justice Cooperation (Eurojust). Eurojust has the mandate to coordinate investigations of serious cross-border crime in Europe and beyond.[a]

Europol's Secure Information Exchange Network Application (SIENA). SIENA offers law enforcement a platform for exchanging crime-related information in the European Union (EU) and with its cooperating partners and third parties with whom it has agreements.[b]

European Investigation Order (EIO). An EIO is a judicial decision issued in or validated by a judicial authority in one EU country in order to use investigative measures to gather or use evidence in criminal matters carried out in another EU country.[c]

European Public Prosecutor's Office (EPPO). The EPPO enables cooperation for investigating, prosecuting, and adjudicating crimes involving the EU budget, such as subsidy fraud and related corruption, as well as cross-border value added tax (VAT) fraud (Wilhelm 2020).

Time-bound formal EIO agreements. These agreements include the Standing Committee on Administrative Cooperation (SCAC) exchanges between EU Member States, which can also enable cooperation between agencies. For example, the SCAC Expert Group in the field of VAT–administrative cooperation enables coordination between Member States to exchange views and discuss and agree on the practical implementation of administrative cooperation in the fight against VAT fraud.[d]

Proposed expansion of EU directive. As of May 2022, a proposal had been made to amend the EU directive on administrative cooperation in the field of taxation with respect to the information sharing with relevant law enforcement agencies. A Member State sending information to another Member State for tax purposes should permit the use of the information for other purposes insofar as it is allowed by the legislation of both Member States. The Member State can do this either by permitting the alternative use after a mandatory request of the other Member State or by communicating to all Member States a list of allowed other purposes.[e]

a. European Union Agency for Criminal Justice Cooperation (Eurojust), https://www.eurojust.europa.eu/about-us. Recently, the Eurojust channel ensured the coordination of investigations at the request of the Italian authorities in a massive cross-border tax fraud scheme (https://www.eurojust.europa.eu/action-counter-italian-fuel-tax-fraud-worth-almost-eur-1-billion).
b. Europol, Secure Information Exchange Network Application (SIENA), https://www.europol.europa.eu/activities-services/services-support/information-exchange/secure-information-exchange-network-application-siena.
c. Eurojust, European Union Agency for Criminal Justice Cooperation, European Investigation Order, https://www.eurojust.europa.eu/judicial-cooperation/eurojust-role-facilitating-judicial-cooperation-instruments/european-investigation-order-eio#:~:text=The%20European%20Investigation%20Order%20(EIO,apply%20in%20Denmark%20and%20Ireland.
d. European Commission, Register of Commission Expert Groups and Other Similar Entities, https://ec.europa.eu/transparency/regexpert/index.cfm?do=groupDetail.groupDetail&groupID=3128&NewSearch=1&NewSearch=1.
e. Proposal for a Council Directive amending Directive 2011/16/EU on administrative cooperation in the field of taxation, COM/2020/314 final, https://eur-lex.europa.eu/legal-content/EN/TXT/?uri=CELEX%3A52020PC0314.

The use of informal methods varies by country, but it is also based on tax or law enforcement attaché relationships, exchange of information with domestic and foreign police/LEAs, and memoranda of understanding on exchange of intelligence. Some countries such as the United States have networks of tax attachés and liaisons that are connected to international criminal investigation offices.

4.3.3 Using MLA in Criminal Matters to Help Tax Recovery

Mutual legal assistance needs a legal basis, such as an undertaking of reciprocity or a bilateral or multilateral agreement. The United Nations Convention against Corruption (UNCAC) is the key multilateral instrument in the context of both prosecution of corruption and money laundering and confiscation and recovery of the proceeds of corruption. Article 46 of UNCAC provides for MLA between competent authorities in investigations, prosecutions, and judicial proceedings for offenses relating to corruption. This assistance includes searches, asset tracing, seizure, freezing, and recovery, among other things. Competent authorities identified by countries under the UNCAC framework include anticorruption agencies, ministries of justice, police, prosecutor's offices, and FIUs.

Some of the instruments recommended by the FATF as important to facilitating international cooperation also include the UN Convention against Illicit Traffic in Narcotic Drugs and Psychotropic Substances and the UN Convention against Transnational Organized Crime (UNTOC). An adequate legal basis for assistance should be made available and treaties, arrangements, or other mechanisms should be in place to enhance cooperation.

Both UNCAC and UNTOC offer the option of using these instruments as the legal basis for an MLA request between countries when no bilateral agreement exists. Information and evidence collected through an MLA request based on either of these two conventions can lead to the discovery of tax violations or fraud, specifically when undisclosed assets are held by offshore shell companies. In this case, the legal framework to exchange information domestically will be vital to authorizing the passage of this information to tax authorities.

Finally, the OECD Forum on Tax and Crime is a platform for government officials involved in combating tax and financial crimes. The objective is to tackle issues at the forefront of the global fight against financial crime and identify practical measures that governments can adopt to ensure interagency implementation of the 10 guiding principles for fighting tax and financial crimes (OECD 2017b).[10] Since its launch in 2011 during the Oslo Dialogue, the forum has held five sessions aimed at improving cooperation and information sharing between government agencies and between countries to prevent, detect, and prosecute financial crime. The Global Tax Crime Law Enforcement Network (GTCLEN), an initiative of the OECD, was scheduled for launch in December 2020, but the meetings were postponed because of the COVID-19 pandemic. The network will provide a platform for investigators, prosecutors, and other tax and financial crime law enforcement officials to meet informally, share experiences and best practices, and establish connections for effective interagency international cooperation.[11]

Notes

1. TIEAs permit competent authorities to engage in the exchange of information on tax matters to assist one another in the administration and enforcement of domestic tax laws.
2. The MCMA is an international treaty designed by the OECD to promote international cooperation between tax authorities on a multilateral basis on various matters, including exchange of information and assistance in collection. The agreement has been signed by 141 jurisdictions. MCMA, http://www.oecd.org/ctp/exchange-of-tax-information/convention-on-mutual-administrative-assistance-in-tax-matters.htm.
3. This agreement supports the automatic exchange of information on a multilateral basis. Overall, 110 countries are signatories to the agreement and have engaged in exchanges. See https://www.oecd.org/tax/automatic-exchange/international-framework-for-the-crs/.
4. These agreements generally facilitate the reciprocal automatic exchange of information, while ensuring that confidentiality and privacy requirements are met.
5. See OECD (2017c), Commentary on Article 26.
6. Council of the European Union, "Joint Investigation Teams: Practical Guide," https://www.europol.europa.eu/sites/default/files/documents/jit-guide-2017-en.pdf.
7. See CARIN, https://www.carin.network/.
8. The Asset Recovery Inter-Agency Network of Southern Africa (ARINSA), Asset Recovery Interagency Network–Asia Pacific (ARIN-AP), Asset Recovery Inter-Agency Network in West and Central Asia (ARIN-WCA), Asset Recovery Inter-Agency Network for the Caribbean (ARIN-CARIB), Asset Recovery Inter-Agency Network for West Africa (ARIN-WA), and Asset Recovery Inter-Agency Network for Eastern Africa (ARIN-EA). Latin America relies on an asset recovery network, Red de Recuperación de Activos de GAFILAT (PRAG), established through GAFILAT, the FATF-style body serving the region.
9. Egmont Group, https://egmontgroup.org/about/.
10. OECD Forum on Tax and Crime, https://www.oecd.org/tax/forum-on-tax-and-crime.htm.
11. OECD Forum on Tax and Crime, https://www.oecd.org/tax/forum-on-tax-and-crime.htm.

References

Eurojust (European Union Agency for Criminal Justice Cooperation). 2002. "Council Framework Decision 2002/465/JHA on Joint Investigation Teams." https://www.eurojust.europa.eu/document/council-framework-decision-2002465jha-joint-investigation-teams.
FATF (Financial Action Task Force). 2011. "FATF's Response to the Public Consultation on the Revision of the FATF Recommendations. FATF, Paris. http://www.fatf-gafi.org/media/fatf/documents/publicconsultation/FATF%20Response%20to%20the%20public%20consultation%20on%20the%20revision%20of%20the%20FATF%20Recommendations.pdf.

IMF (International Monetary Fund). 2012. "Revisions to the Financial Action Task Force Standard—Information Note to the Executive Board." IMF, Washington, DC. https://www .imf.org/external/np/pp/eng/2012/071712a.pdf.

OECD (Organisation for Economic Co-operation and Development). 1998. *Harmful Tax Competition: An Emerging Global Issue*. Paris: OECD. https://www.oecd.org/ctp/harmful /1904176.pdf.

OECD (Organisation for Economic Co-operation and Development). 2012. "Update to Article 26 of the OECD Model Tax Convention and Its Commentary." OECD, Paris. https:// www.oecd.org/ctp/exchange-of-tax-information/120718_Article%2026-ENG_no%20 cover%20(2).pdf.

OECD (Organisation for Economic Co-operation and Development). 2013. *Effective Inter-Agency Cooperation in Fighting Tax Crimes and Other Financial Crimes*. 2d ed. Paris: OECD Publishing. http://www.oecd.org/tax/crime/effective-inter-agency-co-operation -in-fighting-tax-crimes-and-other-financial-crimes-second-edition.pdf.

OECD (Organisation for Economic Co-operation and Development). 2014. *Standard for Automatic Exchange of Financial Account Information in Tax Matters*. Paris: OECD Publishing. http://www.oecd.org/ctp/exchange-of-tax-information/standard-for-automatic-exchange -of-financial-account-information-for-tax-matters-9789264216525-en.htm.

OECD (Organisation for Economic Co-operation and Development). 2017a. *Effective Inter-Agency Cooperation in Fighting Tax Crime and Other Financial Crimes*. 3d ed. Paris: OECD Publishing. https://www.oecd.org/tax/crime/effective-inter-agency-co-operation -in-fighting-tax-crimes-and-other-financial-crimes-third-edition.pdf.

OECD (Organisation for Economic Co-operation and Development). 2017b. *Fighting Tax Crime—The Ten Global Principles*. Paris: OECD Publishing. http://www.oecd.org/tax /crime/fighting-tax-crime-the-ten-global-principles.htm.

OECD (Organisation for Economic Co-operation and Development). 2017c. *Model Tax Convention on Income and on Capital: Condensed Version 2017*. Paris: OECD Publishing. http://dx.doi.org/10.1787/mtc_cond-2017-en.

Wilhelm, Kerstin. 2020. "The European Public Prosecutor's Office—The First Step to a Powerful, Cross-Border Investigation Authority?" *Linklaters* (blog), October 19, 2020. https://www.linklaters.com/en-us/insights/blogs/businesscrimelinks/2020/october /the-european-public-prosecutors-office.

5. Conclusions and Recommendations

This report has described how tax authorities and law enforcement authorities (LEAs) are able to complement one another when they no longer work in silos, which they are still doing in many jurisdictions. Improving their cooperation will lead to progress in the fight against both "regular" financial crime and tax evasion. To improve cooperation between the tax agencies and the LEAs engaged in this effort, countries should consider the following recommendations:

1. Overcome legal barriers to information exchange by

   - Facilitating cooperation through developing a legislative framework formally linking tax crimes to broader financial crimes, particularly by making tax evasion a predicate offense of money laundering and prosecuting such cases;
   - Enacting and implementing legislation authorizing or mandating tax authorities to disclose to prosecutors or LEAs transactions found during tax audits for which there is a reasonable basis to believe that they facilitate the commission of financial crimes;
   - Enacting and implementing legislation authorizing or mandating LEAs to disclose to tax authorities information and evidence found during criminal investigations when there is a reasonable basis to believe that tax evasion is committed;
   - Developing internal standard operating procedures governing the interagency exchange of information, specifying the nature of information to be shared, the time frame, and the exact steps to follow; and
   - Removing legal and administrative barriers to international cooperation between the relevant agencies and the tax authorities and financial intelligence units (FIUs) of counterpart countries.

2. Enhance the availability and collection of pertinent information by

   - Enacting and implementing legal provisions to recover unexplained wealth, illicit enrichment, or unjustified resources to facilitate the recovery of assets and taxes;
   - Ensuring that tax forms for politically exposed persons and their close relatives include questions on whether they submitted asset disclosure forms and ensuring that tax authorities and LEAs can access these forms easily;

- Addressing tax avoidance strategies through mandatory disclosure rules (MDRs) by providing information about the types of structures adopted and striking a balance regarding the potential for disclosure to result in self-incrimination of intermediaries (noncompliance with MDRs should result in the communication of this information to the relevant authorities as well as dissuasive penalties); and
- Introducing beneficial ownership frameworks that
  - Cover all legal arrangements and persons,
  - Align definitions for all agencies obliged to collect relevant information,
  - Require key stakeholders to collect beneficial ownership information and enforce compliance with obligations,
  - Establish a systematic exchange of information between tax authorities and LEAs on beneficial ownership to support cross-verification through information matching, and
  - Develop the use of centralized digital registries that facilitate more cooperation between agencies and identify broad parameters for ascertaining who has effective control over legal persons and legal arrangements.

3. Overcome operational barriers to interagency exchange of information by

- Adopting formal models for cooperation between agencies such as memoranda of understanding, service-level agreements, joint investigative teams or joint task forces, and joint training interventions, among other things;
- Providing the relevant agencies with training on the benefits and available methods of interagency cooperation, making them aware of red flags indicating offenses of interest to counterpart authorities and involving key representatives from each relevant authority in a network of formal and informal relationships;
- Establishing secure systems for communications and exchange of information between agencies and reinforcing the security of platforms, confidentiality, and data protection, including robust measures to avoid the misuse of data;
- Supporting informal channels of cooperation between agencies where ongoing relationships may be established by way of interactions during secondments of staff, use of shared databases, shared intelligence or fusion centers, and joint training sessions;
- Establishing joint task forces to permit ongoing exchange and cooperation in dealing with recurring or larger crimes that involve complex layers or multiple individuals and establishing clear mandates and objectives for the task forces to ensure continued access to the shared expertise; and

- Conducting international investigations using fully integrated and coordinated interagency mechanisms maximizing the use of both informal and formal processes for the exchange of law enforcement and tax information.

4. Overcome cultural and political barriers by

- Balancing efforts to exchange information between tax and law enforcement agencies with confidentiality, privacy, and data protection concerns to promote trust and cultural buy-in; and
- Using all relevant sources of information and international instruments to conduct international cooperation in tax matters and corruption and money laundering investigations.

Countries may also consider

- Introducing laws to expand information gathering possibilities, including those related to mandatory disclosure of the use of aggressive tax avoidance schemes; and
- Adopting unexplained wealth or illicit enrichment laws that could provide authorities with the power to query a person's income or wealth that has no known sources within a sound legal regime and robust good governance framework.

administrative confiscation. A nonjudicial mechanism for confiscating the proceeds of crime or assets used or involved in the commission of an offense.

assets. Entire property of a person, corporation, or estate. Can take the form of corporeal or incorporeal, movable or immovable, tangible or intangible, and legal documents or instruments evidencing title to or interest in such assets.[1] See **property.**

bona fide purchaser. See **innocent owner.**

coercive investigation techniques. Generally, measures that law enforcement authorities can take without the consent of a defendant or a concerned third party by virtue of statutory, judicial, or other authorizations. Examples are searches, electronic surveillance, examination of financial records, access to documents held by third parties, or a production order. A **mutual legal assistance request** is typically required to obtain evidence through coercive techniques.

civil action. See **private law action.**

claimant. The party asserting an interest in an asset or a dispute. The claimant could be a third party, innocent owner, defendant, target, or offender.

commingled assets. The proceeds or instrumentalities of an offense that have been mixed with other assets that may not be the proceeds of a crime.

confiscation. The permanent deprivation of assets by the order of a court or other competent authority.[2] The persons or entities that hold an interest in the specified funds or other assets at the time of the confiscation lose all rights, in principle, to the confiscated funds or other assets.[3] See **forfeiture**.

conviction-based confiscation. All forms of confiscation that require the defendant to be convicted of an offense before confiscation proceedings can be initiated and confiscation can take place.

criminal confiscation. See **conviction-based confiscation.**

defendant. Any party who is required to answer the complaint of a plaintiff in a civil lawsuit before a court, or any party who has been formally charged with or accused of violating a criminal statute.

ex parte proceedings. Legal proceedings brought by one person in the absence of and without the representation or notification of other parties.

financial intelligence unit (FIU). According to the Egmont Group, "[a] central, national agency responsible for receiving, (and as permitted, requesting), analyzing and disseminating to the competent authorities, disclosures of financial information: (i) concerning suspected proceeds of crime and potential financing of terrorism, or (ii) required by national legislation or regulation, in order to combat money laundering and terrorism financing."[4] A more colloquial definition would be a national agency responsible for gathering, analyzing, and disseminating information from financial and related institutions on the suspected proceeds of crimes or the financing of terrorism to combat money laundering and terrorism.

forfeiture. See **confiscation.**

freezing. See **provisional measures.**

gatekeeper. A professional who seeks, either knowingly or unwittingly, to move or conceal the proceeds of illegal activity such as money laundering transactions. Also called facilitators, gatekeepers include accountants, lawyers, financial consultants, or other professionals holding accounts at a financial institution and acting on behalf of their clients. Criminals may seek to use a gatekeeper to access the financial system, while remaining anonymous themselves.

hearsay. An out-of-court statement that is offered in court as evidence to prove the truth of the matter asserted. Whereas civil law jurisdictions do not usually exclude hearsay from proceedings, hearsay is inadmissible in common law jurisdictions (with some exceptions). If hearsay is admitted, the court must also consider the appropriate weight to give the evidence.

informal assistance. Any international cooperation assistance provided without the need for a formal mutual legal assistance (MLA) request. Legislation may permit this type of practitioner-to-practitioner assistance, including MLA legislation.

innocent owner. A third party with an interest in an asset subject to confiscation who did not know of the conduct giving rise to the confiscation. See **bona fide purchaser.**

in personam. "Directed toward a particular person." In the context of confiscation or a lawsuit, it indicates a legal action against a specific person.

in rem. "Against a thing." In the context of confiscation, it indicates a legal action against a specific thing or asset. See **property-based confiscation**.

instrument or instrumentality. An asset used to facilitate crime, such as the car or boat used to transport narcotics or cash.

know your customer. The due diligence and bank regulation that financial institutions and other regulated entities must fulfill to identify their clients and ascertain relevant information pertinent to conducting financial business with them.

letters rogatory. A formal request from a court to a foreign court for some type of judicial assistance. It permits formal communication between the judiciary, a prosecutor, or a law enforcement official of one jurisdiction and his or her counterpart in another jurisdiction. It is a particular form of mutual legal assistance.

mutual legal assistance (MLA). The process by which jurisdictions seek and provide assistance in gathering information, intelligence, and evidence for investigations (through formal channels); in implementing provisional measures; and in enforcing foreign orders and judgments. Assistance can be provided informally (see **informal assistance**) or formally (see **mutual legal assistance request**).

mutual legal assistance (MLA) request. An MLA request is typically a request in writing that must adhere to specified procedures, protocols, and conditions set out in multilateral or bilateral agreements or domestic legislation. These requests are generally used to gather evidence (including through coercive investigative techniques), obtain **provisional measures**, and seek enforcement of domestic orders in a foreign jurisdiction.

nonconviction-based (NCB) confiscation. Confiscation for which a criminal conviction is not required.[5]

open-source intelligence (OSINT). Generally, publicly available information that can be gathered by any legal means, including information available through social media or the internet at no cost, for a fee, or on a subscription basis.

politically exposed persons (PEPs). Individuals who are or have been entrusted with prominent public functions, according to the Financial Action Task Force.

private law action. A legal action by which a person requests the judge to enforce a law and protect his/her rights.

proceeds of crime. Any asset derived from or obtained, directly or indirectly, through the commission of an offense.[6] In most jurisdictions, commingled assets are included.

property. See **assets.**

property-based confiscation. A confiscation action that targets a specific thing or asset found to be the proceeds or instrumentalities of crime. See ***in rem*** and **tainted property**.

provisional measures. Measures temporarily prohibiting the transfer, conversion, disposition, or movement of assets or temporarily assuming custody or control of assets on the basis of an order issued by a court or other competent authority.[7] The term is used interchangeably with **freezing, restraint, seizure,** attachment, and blocking.

requested jurisdiction. A jurisdiction asked to provide assistance to another jurisdiction for the purpose of assisting a foreign investigation or prosecution or enforcing a judgment.

requesting jurisdiction. A jurisdiction asking for the assistance of another jurisdiction for the purpose of assisting with a domestic investigation or prosecution or enforcing a judgment.

restraint. See **provisional measures.**

seizure. See **provisional measures.**

seller for value. See **innocent owner.**

special investigative techniques. Special investigative techniques—such as wiretapping, electronic surveillance, undercover investigations, searches, arrests, and plea bargaining—usually requiring judicial authorization. A **mutual legal assistance request** is typically required for gathering evidence through such techniques in foreign countries. Special investigative tools are specifically used to investigate the most serious crimes, including participation in or leading a criminal organization, trafficking, racketeering, corruption, and money laundering.

state capture. A type of systemic political corruption in which private interests and government officials significantly influence a state's decision-making processes to their own advantage and render accountability mechanisms ineffectual.

substitute assets. Assets that cannot be linked to an offense giving rise to confiscation, but that may be confiscated in substitution for such assets if the assets directly subject to confiscation cannot be located or are otherwise unavailable.

suspicious activity report (SAR). See **suspicious transaction report.**

suspicious transaction report (STR). A report filed by a financial institution about a suspicious or potentially suspicious transaction, whereas a suspicious activity report focuses on the activity rather than a transaction. The report is filed with the jurisdiction's **financial intelligence unit**. See **suspicious activity report**.

tainted property. See **property-based confiscation.**

target or targets. The suspect or suspects of an investigation.

value-based confiscation. A confiscation action to recover the value of benefits that have been derived from criminal conduct and to impose a monetary penalty of an equivalent value.

Notes

1. United Nations Convention against Corruption, art. 2(e).
2. United Nations Convention against Corruption, art. 2(g). See also the Financial Action Task Force (FATF), *Best Practices: Confiscation (Recommendations 3 and 38)*, adopted by the FATF plenary, February 19, 2010.
3. Financial Action Task Force, *Interpretative Note to Special Recommendation III: Freezing and Confiscating Terrorist Assets*, para. 7(c), http://www.fatf-gafi.org/dataoecd/53/32/342 62136.pdf.
4. Definition adopted at the plenary meeting of the Egmont Group, Rome, November 1996; as amended at the Egmont plenary meeting, Guernsey, June 2004.
5. Financial Action Task Force, *Best Practices: Confiscation (Recommendations 3 and 38)*, adopted by the FATF plenary, February 19, 2010.
6. United Nations Convention against Corruption, art. 2(e).
7. Adapted from the United Nations Convention against Corruption, art. 2(f).

Appendix A: Cases

The following cases were identified in the context of a World Bank workshop, as well as from open-source review.

Case 1. The Businessperson and His Hidden Untaxed Assets

Overview. The promoter of a business group had a combined yearly turnover of approximately $16 million.[1] His group consisted of one proprietary concern and three closely held companies operating in the food and fashion sectors. He and his family were suspected of having undisclosed assets abroad not commensurate with their declared income, assets, and profile.

Investigation. Undisclosed assets in foreign countries suspected of belonging to the promoter and his family triggered suspicious transaction reports (STRs). The financial intelligence units (FIUs) in those countries spontaneously shared these reports with the FIU in the promoter's home country, which then shared them with the country's tax authorities. The tax authorities checked the reports against the promoter's and family's declared income and tax payments and found them to be inconsistent. Proceedings against the promoter and family were then launched. The FIU and tax authorities also spontaneously shared these reports with other interested jurisdictions, which began inquiries.

The authorities traced 11 safety deposit lockers to the promoter and his family. They contained undisclosed cash and jewelry valued at over $1.8 million.[2] In addition, the authorities seized mobile phones and deciphered messages indicating that the promoter's family were the beneficial owners of undisclosed offshore entities and foreign assets.

Outcome. The investigation found that the promoter's family owned several undisclosed assets, including (1) three offshore entities incorporated in Belize, the British Virgin Islands, and the Seychelles; (2) bank accounts held in Hong Kong SAR, China; Singapore; Switzerland; and the United States with a balance of $10 million and credits arranged through shell companies, including credit cards from the Swiss bank; (3) real estate in London held through an offshore entity and valued at $5 million, in addition to other substantive real estate holdings; (4) insurance policies in Canada; (5) luxury items and other conspicuous expenses in foreign countries with unaccounted sources of income; and (6) various expenses incurred in foreign countries settled by underinvoicing export proceeds and cash remittances through illegal channels.

Benefits of cooperation. The STRs triggered unexplained wealth investigations resulting in tax recovery in the home country and possible legal consequences in other jurisdictions.

Case 2. The Corrupt Civil Servants and Life Insurance Policies

Overview. Two officials of a country's administrative service, who occupied various posts at various levels over a period of 20 years, had significant undeclared assets and sources of income, notably through a family member. The assets and income were initially uncovered by the tax authorities and subsequently referred to the anticorruption authorities.

Investigation. STRs were received and disseminated by the FIU about the purchase of life insurance policies under suspicious circumstances by individuals who had no explainable source of income. They paid in cash, demanded that drafts be taken from the bank accounts of third parties, and used false names and addresses. These events triggered an investigation by the tax authorities, which resulted in the two public officials admitting to undeclared income of $180,000. Later, the FIU received another STR, this time about an investment of $80,000 in insurance companies by a company owned by the mother of one of the public officials. Later it was revealed that she had no declared source of income. The tax authorities then launched further investigations and ultimately referred the matter to the anticorruption authorities.

Outcome. Searches carried out by the tax authorities identified the following assets tied to the two public officials: (1) over 387 acres of agricultural land, 27 real estate properties, and seven plots valued at $30 million; (2) businesses valued at $2.3 million; (3) $1.3 million held in 77 bank accounts; (4) $410,000 in cash, in addition to foreign currency; and (5) jewelry estimated at $77,000 and liquor estimated at $2,000. As a result, the tax authorities determined the actual income of the two public officials to be $20.8 million and $130,000, respectively.

Benefits of cooperation. The STRs triggered searches by the tax authorities and the identification of undeclared assets of public officials, resulting in referral and the opening of a corruption investigation.

Case 3. The Missing Stone Trader

Overview. The Missing Stone Trader case involves the manipulation of the European Union (EU) value added tax (VAT) system. It is commonly known as transnational Missing Trader Intra-Community (MTIC) fraud. Goods (stones) were moved between EU Member States VAT-free (intracommunity trade) and then sold in a Member State by company A, which charged the buyer, company B, the price of the goods plus the relevant domestic VAT rate. However, company A failed to declare the transactions or pay the VAT tax collected on the sale to the relevant tax authority. Instead, it went "missing" (thus the expression "missing trader") and defaulted on its VAT liability. Company B, and subsequent traders (such as companies C and D) within the Member State, played the role of "buffer traders" and were used to create distance with the missing trader—in this case, company A. Because of the MTIC fraud, the Member State in which these domestic trades were conducted was deprived of the revenue from the VAT owed on the imported goods. Indeed, the MTIC fraud involving the supply of stones from country 1 to countries 2 and 3 defrauded the countries of €27.5 million in VAT.

Investigation. The investigation of the MTIC fraud relied on a high degree of national cooperation to audit the many companies suspected of participating in the scheme, as well as international cooperation between the law enforcement agencies and tax authorities of countries 1, 2, and 3 to investigate payments, invoices, and the transport of goods. In country 1, the investigation relied on 80 officers, who together collected data on 67 fictitious companies, intercepted the communications of the suspected perpetrators, and conducted covert surveillance, notably by using various tracking technologies. The Missing Stone Trader case resulted in 29 searches of commercial and private addresses to seize documents, records, and computers—22 in country 1, five in country 2, and two in country 3.

Outcome. Twenty-six individuals were charged and eight were taken into custody.

Benefits of cooperation. Effective cross-border cooperation and significant criminal investigative resources within and across countries can help tackle VAT MTIC fraud.

Case 4. The Terrorism Financiers

Overview. Foreign nationals were suspected of financing terrorism or operating a business (the construction of a mall) using financing derived from terrorist activities. Although the investigation into the terrorism financing component did not result in usable evidence, the authorities were able to establish that tax offenses had been committed because law enforcement authorities shared information with tax authorities.

Investigation. The tax authorities confirmed that the foreign nationals and the company through which they operated had significant undeclared income and an undeclared tax liability of $3.5 million.

Outcome. The tax authorities sought an asset freeze, and charges were brought against the company directors for tax evasion.

Benefits of cooperation. Sharing of information among competent agencies can enable prosecution in one area (in this case, tax), where prosecution in another area has failed (in this case, terrorism financing).

Case 5. The Divorce Case

Overview. The undeclared offshore holdings of the former managing director of a state-owned electricity utility were uncovered during his divorce proceedings in country A. Foreign authorities in country B then investigated, froze, and later confiscated his assets held in a bank account in country B that were tied to suspected corruption and money laundering.

Investigation. Filings made in divorce proceedings in country A alleged that the former managing director was the beneficial owner of a company incorporated in country B that controlled assets worth several million dollars held in foreign accounts and in the form of real estate. Following a suspicious transaction report, country B authorities investigated the bank accounts in cooperation with foreign counterparts, which revealed that the funds were the proceeds of corruption, specifically bribes that the former official had received from global engineering and energy companies in exchange for valuable contracts with the state electricity utility in country A. The international cooperation component of the investigation included legal assistance from 12 jurisdictions.

Outcome. The country B–registered company pled guilty in a court in country B to laundering the proceeds of corruption between 1999 and 2001, resulting in the confiscation in 2016 of its assets, totaling approximately $4.7 million. Of that, $3.9 million was returned to country A subject to an asset sharing agreement signed in 2017.

Benefits of cooperation. The flow of information from civil proceedings about undeclared offshore accounts to tax authorities triggered investigations into tax evasion and corruption.

Case 6. The Case of Stolen Motor Vehicles

Overview. According to news reports, thousands of stolen vehicles in country A (by one estimate, as many as 80 percent of all stolen vehicles in that country) end up making their way to eastern and central Africa. A particularly popular route is through country B to country C, a common final destination for the stolen vehicles. Criminals often take advantage of discrepancies in customs rules and checks across countries to smuggle the vehicles.

Investigation. Country B authorities opened an investigation into motor vehicles stolen in country A and illegally exported to country C via a port in country B. The scheme was operated by an organized criminal network that fraudulently declared to country B's customs authorities that the vehicles were mattresses, hacked the national vehicle registry, and bribed customs and tax officials in country B's tax authority.

Outcome. Identified as stolen were 124 high-end vehicles, which had been illegally registered. The estimated tax loss to country B was approximately $5 million. Other investigations resulted in similar findings. For example, they revealed 24 stolen vehicles, including high-end Range Rovers, Audis, and BMWs, worth over $1.3 million. The vehicles were recovered and returned to country A.

Benefits of cooperation. Cooperation between law enforcement agencies and tax and customs authorities across countries was essential to finding and recovering the stolen vehicles that were illegally exported.

Case 7. The Globe-Trotting Lobbyist

Overview. A lobbyist acting as an unregistered agent of a foreign government, the government's former president, and the former political party in power colluded in a scheme for almost a decade to hide income from the lobbyist's activities for the purpose of evading taxes. The scheme involved the use of shell companies and foreign bank accounts to disguise income totaling millions of dollars as loans. Later, the lobbyist used his nondeclared assets, notably real estate properties, as collateral to fraudulently secure numerous bank loans amounting to $20 million.

Investigation. Law enforcement agencies in the home country began looking into the activities of the lobbyist following a regime change in the foreign country in 2014. Through cooperation between the financial intelligence unit and law enforcement, the investigation was able to rely on suspicious transaction reports submitted by financial institutions as far back as 2012. They identified the transfer of more than $3 million from 2012 to 2013 between offshore companies linked to the lobbyist.

Outcome. The investigation revealed that more than $75 million flowed through offshore accounts connected to the lobbyist and his activities abroad, with more than $30 million in income concealed from the authorities. As a result, he was indicted and convicted for tax fraud, failure to report foreign bank and financial accounts,[3] and bank fraud. He also pled guilty to related conspiracy charges. As part of his plea agreement, the lobbyist agreed to forfeit $26 million. Following a presidential pardon in December 2020, prosecutors abandoned efforts to seize outstanding assets.

Benefits of cooperation. Cooperation between law enforcement agencies, a tax authority, and a financial intelligence unit resulted in a successful conviction for a large-scale cross-border tax evasion scheme.

Case 8. The Budget Minister

Overview. In December 2012, the press reported that a country's budget minister was holding undeclared assets in bank accounts in Switzerland and Singapore. The minister, who also happened to be the former president of the National Assembly's Finance Commission, had been a vocal proponent of the fight against tax evasion and had repeatedly denied possessing foreign bank accounts.

Investigation. The news report triggered an investigation based on money laundering charges linked to tax evasion. Requests for mutual legal assistance were submitted to Switzerland and Singapore, yielding good results. Swiss authorities confirmed in early 2013 that funds belonging to the budget minister had been held in Swiss bank accounts until 2010, when they were then transferred to bank accounts in Singapore. Furthermore, prosecutors uncovered additional undeclared accounts in the Isle of Man. The minister's total undeclared assets were estimated at €3.5 million.

Outcome. The budget minister admitted that he laundered the proceeds of tax evasion by transferring and holding in Switzerland undeclared revenue from his former activities as a plastic surgeon and owner of a clinic and from his consulting firm. In 2016, he was convicted of tax evasion and money laundering and sentenced to three years in prison. On the basis of the information shared by prosecutors, the tax administration was able to conduct its own administrative case and directly recover €2.3 million in unpaid taxes and penalties from the defendant. The tax proceedings greatly benefited from the prosecutor's decision to launch a money laundering investigation and from the evidence collected through the criminal proceedings.

Benefits of cooperation. Both domestic interagency cooperation and international cooperation resulted in successful and parallel criminal prosecution and tax proceedings.

Case 9. The Crime Boss

Overview. A criminal syndicate operating in country A by a criminal organization from country B was suspected of gold smuggling, drug trafficking, assault, murder, fraud, vehicle cloning, tax evasion, and customs-related offenses. The leader of the criminal organization, Mr. X, once thought to be among the richest men in country B, had fled his home country around 2005 because he was being charged with tax fraud (for which he was found guilty in absentia). After a stay in country C, Mr. X entered country A in 2007 under a fake passport and proceeded to operate a criminal syndicate.

Investigation. In response to domestic requests from law enforcement and tax authorities, country A's financial intelligence unit analyzed transactional data, regulatory reports, personal profiles, property and vehicle databases, and company and intellectual property searches, which enabled it to connect criminal activities to the syndicate run by the organized crime boss, Mr. X. The information was shared with the multiagency task force in charge of the investigation, which included law enforcement agencies as well as the tax authority.

Outcome. The investigation led to the successful prosecution of members of the criminal syndicate, including the organized crime leader, Mr. X, for attempted murder and kidnapping in connection with a drug deal gone wrong, and it resulted in the recovery of approximately $19.6 million in proceeds from crime and related property, including cash, vehicles, boats, firearms, customs seizures, and stolen goods. The revenue services were instrumental in obtaining a court order to preserve the assets of Mr. X and his family and associates on the basis that he owed more than $4 million in taxes, penalties, and interest.

Benefits of cooperation. Effective cooperation between the tax agency and law enforcement agencies resulted in the successful confiscations.

Case 10. The Payroll Services Company

Overview. A criminal syndicate was using a payroll services company to perpetrate a large-scale tax fraud conspiracy. The payroll services company, which was concentrating heavily on the information technology industry, diverted pay-as-you-go withholding taxes and goods and services taxes, thereby defrauding the country in which it was located of more than $79 million in revenue over a period of three years.

Investigation. The investigation began in 2016, triggered by a routine tax inquiry by the taxation authority into the "phoenix" arrangements in the labor hire or outsourcing industry, the area in which the payroll services company operated. "Phoenixing" refers to a practice in which companies with outstanding debts, including a tax liability, are liquidated to avoid having to pay their debts. When the complexity of the scheme became apparent, the investigation was taken over by the police with support from the tax authority under the umbrella of a serious financial crime task force. The task force, established in 2015, deals with the most serious and complex forms of financial crimes by making use of the intelligence and specialist powers of its member agencies. It is composed of the police, attorney general, financial intelligence unit, securities commission, and public prosecutors, among others.

Outcome. The investigation culminated in a series of raids in May 2017. Through a criminal assets confiscation task force, the authorities recovered an estimated $12 million in assets linked to the founder of the payroll services company, including six properties, three vehicles, multiple bank accounts, investment accounts, shareholdings, and luxury items. The investigation resulted in charges brought against 16 individuals, and a number of them were convicted and sentenced to prison.

Benefits of cooperation. Long-standing task forces that bring together agencies can join to undertake effective investigations of complex, large-scale criminal schemes.

Notes

1. The $16 million corresponds to the turnover in fiscal 2013–14.
2. Unless otherwise specified, current exchange rates were used to convert local currencies to approximate values in US dollars.
3. In the concerned jurisdiction, if a resident or national controls a foreign bank account worth at least $10,000, he or she is required to file a foreign bank and financial account report and income tax forms declaring any foreign account holdings. Failure to do so is a tax crime.

www.ingramcontent.com/pod-product-compliance
Lightning Source LLC
Chambersburg PA
CBHW041448210326
41599CB00004B/181